UNDERSTANDING
REVELATION

IHERINGIUS

Copyright © 2021 by Marko Joensuu

The moral right of the author has been asserted.

Unless otherwise stated, all Bible quotations are taken from the *New Revised Standard Version* (NRSV).

All rights reserved.
No part of this publication may be reproduced, stored in a retrieval system, or transmitted, in any form or by any means, without the prior permission in writing of the publisher, nor be otherwise circulated in any form of binding or cover other than that in which it is published and without a similar condition including this condition being imposed on the subsequent publisher.

ISBN 978-1-9164811-5-2

A CIP catalogue record for this book is available from the British Library.

Iheringius
An imprint of
Joensuu Media Ltd
20-22 Wenlock Road
London
N1 7GU
England

www.iheringius.com

UNDERSTANDING
REVELATION

MARKO JOENSUU

Come, Lord Jesus!

CONTENTS

Acknowledgements	9
Introduction	11
Brief Outline	27
Revelation 1	31
Revelation 2	53
Revelation 3	85
Revelation 4	97
Revelation 5	101
Revelation 6	107
Revelation 7	113
Revelation 8	117
Revelation 9	121
Revelation 10	127
Revelation 11	129
Revelation 12	137
Revelation 13	141
Revelation 14	175
Revelation 15	183
Revelation 16	187
Revelation 17	191
Revelation 18	201
Revelation 19	207
Revelation 20	211
Revelation 21	219
Revelation 22	225

Bibliography	229
Historical Sources	233
Other Books by Marko Joensuu	235

ACKNOWLEDGEMENTS

The libraries of two institutions—Tampere University and the British Library—have been instrumental in my research for this book.

I have benefited immensely from working towards my doctorate in journalism, as there is an overlap in methodology of researching texts between my research approach and study of biblical texts. And my earlier studies in history and historical methods at Tampere University have served me well.

I thank God for the longsuffering of my wife Daniella, as researching for this book and writing it has taken a lot of time. I am also thankful for the creativity of my son Joshua; he has always inspired me.

Writing this book has been a lonely endeavour, and most of my conversations have been conducted with books and articles by New Testament scholars and historians.

I thank God for His continual strengthening and for His guidance, as putting this book together has demanded reliance on nearly every discipline I have ever studied. Also, my ministry has been prophetic in nature, and understanding the language of dreams and visions has been helpful in the process of attempting to understand Revelation.

I have not looked for any endorsements. Soren Kierkegaard, one of the theologians and philosophers that has impacted me the most, once penned that he wrote "without authority". Ultimately, it is the text that needs to be able to persuade the reader rather than the earthly position of the author.

INTRODUCTION

For a long time, I considered Revelation to be practically an indecipherable book that would finally be explained by the very last end-time events within a short final time span on the final page of human history. It was the last book in the Bible, after all, I reasoned.

I had given up on trying to decipher it in the late 1980s and found the words of the Danish theologian and philosopher Soren Kierkegaard (1990, 29) practical and useful:

> "But," your perhaps say, "there are so many obscure passages in the Bible, whole books that are practically riddles." To that I would answer: Before I have anything to do with this objection, it must be made by someone whose life manifests that he has scrupulously complied with all the passages that are easy to understand: is this the case for you? Yet this is how the lover would respond to the letter—if there were obscure passages but also clearly expressed wishes, he would say, "I must immediately comply with the wish—then I will see about the obscure parts. How could I ever sit down and ponder the obscure passages and not comply with the wish, the wish that I clearly understood." In other words, when you are reading God's word, it is not the obscure passages that bind you but what you understand, and with that you are to comply at once.

There is so much in the Bible that is clear and actionable, and I had enough trouble with Jesus's clear commandments to devote myself to a book that many theologians have tried to decipher in vain for centuries, with those seemingly certain about its exact meaning mostly proven wrong within their own lifetime.

The defining moment came in the mid-1980s, when a well-known end-times teacher seemed certain that the birthmark on the then Soviet President Mikhail Gorbachev's forehead was the mark of the beast and predicted that in the coming year Gorbachev would take over the world as the Antichrist. This was because, allegedly, his birthmark resembled the world map. If it happened, it happened so secretly that we missed it, and the Soviet Union collapsed some years later without the prophesied communist world takeover. In later years, I have been able to facilitate mission in the fragments of the lost Soviet empire, and Russia has receded in the minds of most Christians as a potential birthplace of the Antichrist. But Gorbachev has proved to have been able to live a healthy and long life, so the end-times expert in question was able to peddle a theory of his return for quite a few years. No apology for the failed prophecy followed, only a steady stream of new theories about the potential identity of the Antichrist, designed for everyone to forget the failed prophecy and to make some money in the process.

Whole libraries could be filled with clearly failed predictions about the identity of the Antichrist. After all, this speculation about it began already in the second century.

Nearly every Christian has come across theories regarding who or what the beast in Revelation might be. During the days of the Cold War, the Soviet Union was everyone's favourite beast. Since then, many have predicted that the Antichrist would come from the EU, China, the Middle East, or the US, with the multimillion-selling *Left Behind* novel series popularising the idea about a Romanian Antichrist, who becomes the UN Secretary General. Consequently, there are millions of Christians around the world expecting the Antichrist to appear to lead a world government, and because of that, millions of evangelical Christians, especially in America, oppose any global cooperation, some even international aid and charity work.

Revelation has entered the popular culture, with novels and movies borrowing from the Apocalypse, often with great artistic freedom. For example, in the beginning of *Pale Rider*, a Western starring Clint Eastwood, a character called the Preacher arrives in a village on

INTRODUCTION

horseback at the precise moment when a young woman is reading the KJV version of Revelation 6:8, which says,

> And I looked, and behold a pale horse: and his name that sat on him was Death, and Hell followed with him.

What follows is a slightly mystical revenge Western where the identity of the Preacher is never fully revealed.

I can remember discussing the finer details of Revelation with a Satanist, a fellow student of journalism, whilst waiting at the reception lounge of the largest newspaper in Finland, with the rest of the students and our professor intently listening to our conversation, looking perplexed. This Satanist had a remarkable interest in Revelation, even when he did not believe in the existence of either God or Satan.

At the time, Revelation seemed to have very little significance to my spiritual growth, and talking about it seemed to lead to endless arguments. In fact, the conversation I had about it with the Satanist has been amongst the most civilised of them all. The apparent ambiguity of Revelation appeared to make almost any interpretation possible but not provable.

And yet many Christians are studying it, and its different interpretations continue to shape global politics. For example, the rise of the Islamic State was energised by an Islamic reinterpretation of the battle of Armageddon referred to in Revelation.

In the Islamic eschatology, Dabiq in Syria is one of the two possible locations for a future epic battle between invading Christians and the defending Muslims, which in the Islamic eschatology will result in the Muslim victory. In this battle, the Muslims would be outnumbered, but Allah would give them victory.

This apocalyptic rationale behind the Islamic State's appeal was lost to most Westerners, but it explains why many of the terrorist group members keep on fighting even when their caliphate has been lost: according to Islamic false prophecy, this battle was never supposed to be easy, with Allah coming to their help only when the Muslim soldiers would be under siege at the eve of destruction.

This Islamic false prophecy borrowed from Revelation and from other biblical prophetic books, but it then repurposed them to serve

UNDERSTANDING REVELATION

Islam. The early Muslims incorporated Jesus into their teaching to ease conversion from Islam to Christianity. If Jesus were one of the Islamic prophets—in a sense, even more special than Muhammed, as it is Jesus and not Muhammed that will return in the end of time according to Islam—then converting from Christianity to Islam would be easier. And the Middle East had large Christian populations before Islam, so incorporating Jesus into the Islamic narrative would have been a major converting strategy.

Jalal al-Din *al Suyuti* (1446-1505) was one of the most important interpreters of the *hadith* (the sayings of Muhammed) predicting the apocalypse. He placed considerable importance on one *hadith*:

> The Hour will not come so long as groups within my community will not have joined with the polytheists, going so far as to worship idols. In my community there will be a succession of thirty imposters, each one pretending to be a prophet. (Filiu 2011, 45)

It is because of these kinds of predictions that Islamic extremists often see Muslims that do not follow their brand of Islam as legitimate targets for execution. They are perceived as people who have left the "real Islam" and apostates. Also, any cooperation between the governments in the predominantly Muslim countries and the West can be interpreted as fulfilment of this prophecy.

Al-Suyuti adopts the classical Islamic traditions concerning the Antichrist and that he would be denied access to the holy cities of Islam—Mecca and Medina. According to Al-Suyuti, the trial because of the Antichrist will be horrendous. But then the Mahdi will appear to restore true Islam for the period of seven years—according to Al-Suyuti, before Jesus, who will come to approve the work of the Mahdi. Jesus will descend on the white minaret in Damascus, chase the Antichrist and kill him at the gate of Lod, before abolishing all other religions but Islam. Al-Suyuti says about Jesus: "He will destroy the cross, he will kill the swine, he will make harmony reign, and he will drive out enmity." (ibid., 45-46)

Al-Suyuti forecast that the Hour would not come any later than AD 2076. Because of this prediction, his influence has never been greater than today. Because of Al-Suyuti and many other Islamic

INTRODUCTION

predictors of the Apocalypse, the violence of the Islamic State has been legitimised in many parts of the Islamic world, as the world is supposed to be a violent and horrendous place before the end of days. (ibid., 47) It is the Islamic repurposing of Revelation that will ensure that the future decades are likely to continue to be violent in many parts of the Middle East.

Both Shia and Sunni apocalyptic thinkers predict that there will be a falling away from Islam—and brutal violence between the Islamic sects, and against the Byzantium, the Eastern Roman Empire that the early Muslims fought against for centuries—which is now reinterpreted to be the West of today. Many of these apocalyptic prophecies also predict a confrontation between the Muslims and the Jews, and the wiping out of the Jews. (ibid., 44-48)

But it is not just Muslims that have repurposed the message of Revelation to their ends. For example, Revelation has had a huge impact on the American foreign policy, even when the politicians applying it might not ever had studied it at all.

Seven Blessings of Reading Revelation

Misinterpreting and misapplying Revelation has brought many curses on earth, yet reading it is promised to bring us many blessings. Revelation contains seven specific blessings for those who remain obedient to Jesus.

Revelation 1:3 promises that "Blessed *is* he who reads and those who hear the words of this prophecy, and keep those things which are written in it."

According to *Revelation 14:13*, blessed are those who die in the Lord, as they will rest from their work, and their good works will follow them to eternity.

According to *Revelation 16:15*, blessed are those who stay awake and remain clothed.

According to *Revelation 19:9*, blessed are those who are invited to the wedding supper of the Lamb.

According to *Revelation 20:6*, blessed are those who share in the first resurrection—the resurrection of the Christians.

According to *Revelation 22:7*, blessed is the one who keeps the words written in Revelation.

UNDERSTANDING REVELATION

And, according to *Revelation 22:14*, blessed are those who wash their robes, because they will enjoy the Tree of Life and enter New Jerusalem.

Many Christians associate Revelation with the figure of the Antichrist, but in fact, the Antichrist is not mentioned in Revelation at all. But they link the person behind 666, the number of the beast, mentioned in *Revelation 13:18*, to the Antichrist, making him some sort of final and evil end-time world ruler.

But I do not think that this interpretation can be easily justified. The reason is that the only books in the Bible that use the word "antichrist" are *1* and *2 John*. If you accept that the author of Revelation is the same apostle John who also wrote John's letters in the New Testament, you will be faced with a major dilemma, as John seems to refute the teaching about one Antichrist as an end-time world ruler in his letters. He writes in *1 John 2:18-19*:

> Children, it is the last hour! As you have heard that antichrist is coming, so now many antichrists have come. From this we know that it is the last hour. They went out from us, but they did not belong to us; for if they had belonged to us, they would have remained with us. But by going out they made it plain that none of them belongs to us.

In his letters, John gives us a very different definition of an antichrist than most Christians who are searching for the Antichrist today. For John, an antichrist is a false teacher who used to be part of a Christian community.

How could John define an antichrist as a false teacher in his letters and then proceed to present one Antichrist as an end-time world leader in Revelation—but without ever using that term? Many liberal scholars would argue that the book, the letters, and the Gospel all have different authors, but I do not think we need to make that conclusion.

And there is no reason to make an effort to save the idea of one Antichrist, as historical context makes it quite clear that John was responding in his letters to a present threat in the minds of many Christians. What he was refuting was a teaching about the Roman emperor as the Antichrist.

INTRODUCTION

Josephus, a Jewish historian, who led the Jewish forces against the Romans in Galilee in the beginning of the First Jewish-Roman War (AD 66-73), which led to the destruction of the Second Temple in Jerusalem, writes in *The Jewish War* (6.5.4.312) about messianic prophecies that stirred the rebellion:

> At about that time, one from their country would become ruler of the habitable world.

At this point, Josephus had already switched on to the Roman side, and he was explaining the Roman victory some years after the destruction of the Second Temple. It appears that he had become disillusioned about the messianic prophecies and was actively repurposing them for the Roman use. So, Josephus, a Jew, loses his faith in the Jewish messianic project after he had been captured by the Romans in Judea. He then makes the claim that this messiah that the Jews were still expecting was in fact the general Vespasian who would be proclaimed the emperor whilst in Judea. It was Vespasian's son Titus who would destroy Jerusalem and the Second Temple, whilst Vespasian would return to Rome to become the emperor, "fulfilling" the prophecy about the world ruler coming out of Judea.

According to Eusebius (*Church History*, Book III, Chapter 12), Vespasian then ordered all descendants of the royal line of David to be hunted down to ensure that no one else could claim this prophecy.

This is the beginning of the *antichrist myth;* it seems that Vespasian harnessed Josephus's lucky prediction about him becoming the emperor to be used as propaganda.

This has also been documented by the Roman historians. Suetonius writes in *The Life of Twelve Caesars: Life of Vespasian* 5.6 about Vespasian in Judea:

> When he consulted the oracle of the god of Carmel in Judaea, the lots were highly encouraging, promising that whatever he planned or wished however great it might be, would come to pass; and one of his high-born prisoners, Josephus by name, as he was being put in chains, declared most confidently that he would soon be released by the same man, who would then, however, be emperor.

UNDERSTANDING REVELATION

Over the next few years, the myth about one ruler that would rise in Judea would spread over the whole Roman Empire. What John is saying in *1 John 2:18-19* is that the Christians have heard that an Antichrist—the Roman emperor—has come. But John is refuting the whole idea that the emperor would be the Antichrist. Instead, what he is saying is that the many antichrists in the world are in fact false teachers who have once been part of the Christian community.

1 John 2:22 says:

> Who is a liar but he who denies that Jesus is the Christ? He is antichrist who denies the Father and the Son.

The recipients of the letter were waiting for one political Antichrist; instead, there would be many theological antichrists. It seems that the apostle John perceived false teachers to be much more detrimental to the Church than persecution by the whole Roman Empire.

Is it not rather odd that John does not mention an antichrist at all in Revelation—the most prophetic book of the New Testament—but he mentions him in a letter written to his contemporaries where he seems to argue against one Antichrist? This should inspire us to study the Scriptures more seriously.

What seems clear is that over the centuries, Christians around the world have projected their fears onto Revelation, so much so that their interpretations often seem to reflect their time and culture more than the contents of Revelation itself.

Over time, these interpretive frameworks have diversified, and academic views on Revelation can be rather different from the interpretations generated by fundamentalist preachers. Today, many scholars seek to explain Revelation as merely a product of its time and the genre conventions the author had in his disposal. But many evangelical writers perceive the book as prophesying what is yet to come, with practically all its content referring to the end-times.

The main frameworks of interpretation are *historicist,* which sees Revelation as a broad view of history, *preterist,* which sees the book mostly referring to the first century or time until the fall of the Roman Empire, *futurist,* which sees Revelation as focused on the final days,

INTRODUCTION

and *idealist* or *symbolic*, which interprets the book as an allegorical battle between good and evil, with no major reference points to real world events.

I do not think that any of these interpretive frameworks manage to explain the contents of Revelation wholly and satisfactorily, although all of them have something to offer. But they all seek to impose a consistent external order to the text, an order that is alien to its internal arrangement. They stop wrestling with the symbols and mysteries of Revelation far too early in their attempt to fit the content of the book in their interpretive model.

Some time ago I set myself a task of reading Revelation differently. I did not begin with a Bible commentary. Commentaries abound, so we can easily rely on them more than on the actual book. In fact, many books seeking to explain Revelation turn out to be studies of commentaries rather than the book itself.

Instead, I resorted to reading Revelation repeatedly over months in a disciplined way by not using any external sources at all, unless Revelation itself clearly pointed at them. But when Revelation clearly pointed beyond itself, I followed the reference.

Then I read books and academic articles that focus on the history and archaeology of the first-century Asia Minor, Rome, and Judea. Many of them do not refer to Revelation at all but give a picture of the culture, history, and religious beliefs of Asia Minor at the time of Revelation's writing, either through written documents or archaeological digs.

Eventually, I concluded that Revelation itself provides a consistent interpretive framework for itself, which, with some help of knowing history and trust in the validity of biblical prophecy, manages to explain itself rather well.

I have approached Revelation with the hermeneutical perspective common in the study of history and theology. Hans-Georg Gadamer is considered the father of *philosophical hermeneutics* and one of the most important philosophical voices of the twentieth century. Gadamer examined the ways historical and cultural circumstances influence human understanding, and he remains popular amongst many theologians, mainly as hermeneutics itself was birthed out of the need for biblical interpretation.

UNDERSTANDING REVELATION

Many people are aware of the concept of the hermeneutical spiral or circle, but they might not know what it means. In hermeneutics, a text is seen as a unity when it comes to its meaning. The individual parts explain the whole, and the whole is explained by the individual parts. Interpretation consists of continual movement from the whole to the part and from the part to the whole, and this process gradually increases and deepens our understanding.

According to Gadamer, someone trying to understand a text is "always projecting." We project a meaning on the text as soon as an initial meaning begins to emerge. This fore-projection is constantly revised, and in every revision round we project a new projection of meaning: rival projects of interpretation can emerge side by side, until it becomes clearer what the unity of meaning is. If the fore-projection is correct, it is confirmed by the text. The art of interpretation is to examine the legitimacy of the "fore-meanings" dwelling within us. (Gadamer 2013, 279-280)

Essentially, we seek to let the text itself to be the judge of our fore-meanings rather than only look for evidence for whatever theory we hold about the text.

But far too often, we are impatient with the text, and when we read a book full of symbolism and metaphors, such as Revelation, we can project our interpretation onto it too quickly. For example, a prominent Bible study site interprets the "beast rising out of the sea" in *Revelation 13:1* to be the Antichrist. But is this interpretation consistent with what Revelation itself reveals about the beast? Is it consistent with the way the Bible defines a beast?

We will proceed from part—one verse—to the whole: from Revelation to the totality of the Bible. And we will soon discover that in the Bible, beasts tend to be empires rather than individuals. Revelation is continuation of the Book of Daniel, and to Daniel, beasts are empires. This means that a theory about the beast in *Revelation 13:1* being the Antichrist is probably wrong, because a beast is an empire and not a person. But now our understanding of the whole has already affected our interpretation of *Revelation 13:1*. If empires are beasts in Daniel, then the beast rising out of the sea must be an empire.

We let Revelation itself explain an individual verse, and then we let the individual verse explain Revelation. Then we let the rest of the

INTRODUCTION

Bible explain the individual verse and Revelation, and vice versa. And we can also, to certain extent, let historical events explain Revelation, as some passages clearly depict events that have already passed in time of writing, and others predict events that have now clearly come to pass. When Revelation was written, they were prophecy. Now they are history. The hermeneutical process can be extended beyond the text to its reference points in the world.

Do you ever mentally skip a Bible verse because you already "know" what it means? This is an example of fore-projecting an interpretation. When we do that we no more let the Bible confront and challenge us, but we have categorised that verse in our mind as a "solved problem", and it does not bother us anymore. This way, the Bible has lost some of its power in our lives.

Over the years, I have tried to read the Bible in different translations and languages, as the resulting sense of unfamiliarity forces me to re-ponder the text's meaning, and I am less able to fore-project an interpretation effortlessly.

Interpretive Guidelines

Following hermeneutical principles, I would suggest following these interpretive guidelines when you study Revelation.

1. Revelation gives plenty of guidance on how to interpret itself. It is the first place to look when explaining it.

For example, in *Revelation 10:2*, a mighty angel comes down from heaven and holds a little scroll in his hand. It should be clear to a careful reader that a little scroll begins a new prophecy.

Revelation 1:8 says that God is the Alpha and the Omega, the Beginning and the End. This implies that Revelation majors in beginnings and endings.

Revelation 1:1 says that the book is about what "must soon take place." Then in *Revelation 4:1*, a voice says to John: "Come up here, and I will show you things which must take place after this."

So, Revelation is not just about beginning and endings, but also about things that will happen soon after John has seen the visions.

But in *Revelation 1:19* Jesus says to John: "Now write what you have seen, what is, and what is to take place after this."

UNDERSTANDING REVELATION

Putting this all together, it seems clear that part of Revelation concerns of things which had already happened at the time John saw the visions. These belong to the things which *are*.

So, Revelation *interprets* the past and how we got where John was at the time of seeing the visions.

Revelation tells about events that were happening at the time John saw the visions. These also belong to the things which *are*.

Revelation predicts what is about to happen. And then it predicts what will happen after what is about to happen. These belong to things that *will take place* after the time of seeing the vision. And then it predicts events which will happen in the end-times.

Based on this, much of Revelation would already have taken place within John's lifetime, and some of it quite soon after that. This might challenge your understanding of Revelation, but that is what Jesus says Himself in Revelation.

For some, a thought that a book of prophecy might explain the past might seem contradictory. But it is not. Revelation gives us God's perspective on the purpose of all time. God is the Great Storyteller, and He knows that for us to understand what will happen, we need to understand what has already taken place, and how we got where we are.

But we should not lose sight of *Revelation 1:1*, which says that the book concerns of what must soon take place. This means that the main emphasis of the book is prophetic and not simply reinterpreting the past or the present, and that many developments shown should begin shortly after John seeing the visions.

2. The first reference point outside Revelation is the Old Testament.
Scholars have counted over two hundred references in Revelation to the Old Testament texts (Lo 1999, 2-3). Most of these are references to the Old Testament's prophetic books. Altogether, there might be over five hundred allusions to the Old Testament.

This means that it would be foolish to study Revelation without also studying the Old Testament. With so many references to the Old Testament, Revelation clearly invites us to study the Jewish Bible. It is the Old Testament, rather than the New Testament, which functions as the main reference point. The reason for this is clear: the New Testament canon had not been compiled at the time

INTRODUCTION

of writing. Although most books and letters ending up as part of the New Testament would already have been written, they would not have been widely available.

But Revelation goes a lot further than that. It is evident that John sees Revelation as a continuation of the work of the Old Testament prophets, even the summary and the explainer of it. Revelation contains new predictive prophecies, but it also explains the Old Testament prophecies.

Revelation makes references to nearly all prophetic books in the Old Testament, and each reference is an invitation to read not just the exact reference but also the surrounding verses. These references function much like hyperlinks, so that we should read Revelation by going back and forth from Revelation to the Old Testament books if we need more clarity.

By and large, Revelation is a book that expands, explains, and continues the Old Testament prophecy. For example, when it comes to the beast, Revelation continues from where Daniel ends.

As Revelation relies so heavily on the Old Testament prophetic books, a sensible approach would be to assess whether it also follows their structure. For example, Jeremiah is structured cyclically as a series of gradually developing wailings about Jerusalem's impending destruction, so its prophecies are not sequenced chronologically but hermeneutically, as Jeremiah seeks to understand the first shocking revelation and his own call, which leads him to a deeper understanding. So, it would be a mistake to read Jeremiah as a singular chronologically structured prophecy. The same applies to Revelation.

3. Symbolism in Revelation follows the conventions developed by the Old Testament prophetic books.

Revelation is a profoundly symbolic book, but there are no randomly chosen symbols. There is very little in the book that is literal, and at the same time, it does refer to real historical events.

Revelation is not one chronological account of world events. In fact, it contains multiple visions of the past, present, and future, looked at from different perspectives.

To understand Revelation, you must seek to understand prophetic language, principles, and visionary symbolism. Here my approach is not entirely scholarly, as my ministry and gifting in this area have somewhat directed my interpretation. But unless you understand the language of dreams and visions, it is very hard to understand a book full of visions. But this does not entitle us to haphazard interpretations. These interpretations must still be supported by the Scriptures, reasonability, and history.

According to Bailey, prophetic literature can use forms such as step parallelism, inverted parallelism, and ring composition (2011, 40-42) in short passages of Scripture. We do not need to get too technical here; the main point is that prophetic writing is not always written chronologically, but the following verses can reinforce the message of the previous verses rather than account events in linear or chronological fashion.

As a journalist, I am used to writing articles that do not outline the narrative in chronological order but move back and forth temporally to reinforce an argument, with the headline often working both as a premise and a conclusion. So, non-chronological ordering of texts should not be unfamiliar to anyone who reads the news.

4. Interpretation of symbols should be consistent and not haphazard.

The symbolic system of Revelation is not haphazard but precise. Yet many scholars and Bible teachers interpret the symbols haphazardly. For example, when *Revelation 7:3* refers to the seal of God on the forehead of His servants, most readers would interpret this to be an invisible seal. Yet, when Revelation *13:16-18* speaks about the mark of the beast, many expect this mark to be a physical mark. That is not consistent but haphazard interpretation of symbols. It does not conform with the symbolic system of Revelation. In fact, from the beginning to the end of the book, Revelation is painstakingly building a complex but consistent symbolic system, and this system is meant to guide a reader's interpretation of the book.

5. The next reference point after the Old Testament prophets should be the rest of the Old Testament and the New Testament.

For example, when in *Revelation 15:3* the saints sing the Song of Moses, it refers to the Song of Moses in *Deuteronomy 32*. To establish

INTRODUCTION

the meaning of the Song of Moses in Revelation, the most sensible thing to do is to read *Deuteronomy 32* first.

But John is also writing to congregations that would have been at least reasonably familiar with Paul's teaching, as Paul established the church of Ephesus. Hence Paul's letters to Asia Minor can often give us useful contextual information and clues.

This referencing to the Old Testament is deeply ingrained in Revelation. As early as in the third century, Dionysius of Alexandria complained about John's poor use of Greek, saying that he employed barbarous idioms. But many irregularities occur because Revelation carries over the exact grammatical form of the Old Testament wording, with this intended dissonance being used as a literary technique to get the reader to see the Old Testament connection more clearly. (Beale 1999, 318-321)

6. You cannot understand Revelation without some knowledge of history.

If Revelation is the book of the Alpha and the Omega, the beginnings and the endings, and what happens between, you will not be able to understand it without at least some understanding of history. How do you separate what has already happened from what is yet to happen, unless you know what has already happened?

As the Old Testament prophecies about the destruction of Israel and Judah demonstrate, God cares deeply about every generation, and not just about ours. Not every Bible prophecy is a prophecy about the end-times, with many Bible prophecies already being fulfilled in the time of Jesus.

7. You cannot understand Revelation unless you acknowledge that at least some of its content is prophecy.

Revelation is a profoundly prophetic book. Much of the historical study of it assumes that there is no actual prophecy in it with scholars perceiving it merely as a symbolic commentary of John's own time. But although our understanding of the first century history is extremely useful, it fails to explain the whole of Revelation.

Paul Ricouer, a French philosopher, saw the Bible as "the grandiose plot of the history of the world", and each literary plot as a "sort of miniature version of the great plot that joins Apocalypse and Genesis". (Ricouer 1985, 23)

But the Apocalypse is yet to happen, which has certain consequences.

According to Ricouer, the Apocalypse, in this respect, offers the model of a prediction that is continually invalidated without ever being discredited, hence of an end that is itself constantly put off. Moreover, and by implication, the invalidation of the prediction concerning the end of the world has given rise to a truly qualitative transformation of the apocalyptic model. From being imminent, it has become immanent. The Apocalypse, therefore, shifts its imagery from the last days, the days of terror, of decadence, of renovation, to become a myth of crisis. (ibid., 23)

This sense of an imminent crisis is the ethos of how many Christians approach Revelation. But this ethos does not help us to understand it. Many Christians project this ethos of an imminent crisis onto any new crisis in their time and believe that this new crisis would somehow be the fulfilment of prophecies in Revelation. This is because all they know about Revelation is a sense of a world in crisis, and now their world appears to be in crisis, which must in their minds mean that they are seeing the prophecies regarding the end-times fulfilled.

BRIEF OUTLINE

Most traditional sources date the writing of Revelation to the reign of the Roman Emperor Domitian (AD 81–96). We will take this estimate as our starting point. But it is likely that some visions might have been revealed to John earlier than that. What seems evident is that Revelation has been written after the destruction of the Second Temple in Jerusalem in AD 70.

Like the Old Testament prophetic books, Revelation does not follow a strict chronological structure, but it is a series of visions that partially overlap and show world events from different perspectives.

Jeremiah is a series of wailings about Jerusalem's impending destruction. Revelation's vision cycle focuses on the Church, Israel, the invisible spiritual dimension, and world history.

This book is not a verse-by-verse commentary, but it follows the structure of Revelation closely. To make full use of it, it is vital that you read it with a Bible next to you. All the Bible references in this book are from the NRSV translation of the Bible, but keeping any translation at hand will be useful.

Revelation was not originally divided into chapters and verses, but as with the rest of the Bible, the chapter and verse numbers were added in the Middle Ages. They are the most convenient way to refer to different parts of the book, but it is good to remember that they can break the text in wrong places and occasionally conceal its message.

UNDERSTANDING REVELATION

Revelation 1 introduces the book as the revelation of Jesus. It also introduces the Church as the main agent of God on earth. Hidden in it is a prophecy about the end-time Israel.

Revelation 2-3 critiques the beginnings of the Early Church but from a prophetic perspective. These chapters do not just describe the situation at the time but project future developments.

Revelation 4 describes heavenly worship and gives a spiritual vision of the universe.

Revelation 5 presents the crucifixion and resurrection of Jesus as the most important events not just in human story but as the decisive moments shaping the nature of the ultimate reality, including heaven.

Revelation 6 maps time from the resurrection of Jesus to the beginning of the end-time judgments.

Revelation 7 presents the saved in the end-times, including the remnant of Israel.

Revelation 8-9 presents physical and spiritual end-time judgments.

Revelation 10 presents a hidden prophecy, which means that Revelation does not claim to reveal everything. It also indicates a shift to a new prophecy about the nations and Israel.

Revelation 11 presents the judgment of Israel through the First Jewish-Roman War but also prophesies the end-time re-emergence of Israel as a political entity.

It blows the seventh trumpet of judgment and merges the story of Israel with the end-time judgments for all nations.

Revelation 12 retells the judgment of Israel as an outcome of Satan trying to kill the Child. It also explains why Satan, the dragon, wars against the Church.

Revelation 13 presents the emergence of the Roman Empire as fulfilment of a prophecy in the Book of Daniel, and it continues Daniel's prophecy.

It presents the development of the prostitute Church as the second beast that supports the world-destroying empire-project of the sinful man.

Revelation 14 presents the remnant of Israel, Rome's coming destruction, and the two harvests—one for souls and another for judgment.

Revelation 15-16 returns to the narrative of the end-time judgments.

BRIEF OUTLINE

Revelation 17 describes the evolution of the second beast into the prostitute Church.

Revelation 18 predicts the destruction of the prostitute Church.

Revelation 19 foretells the beginning of the heavenly wedding and Christ overcoming all spiritual and physical opposition.

Revelation 20 presents the thousand-year rule of Christ on earth as the fulfilment of prophecies about the restoration of Israel, the following rebellion, and the final judgment of Satan.

Revelation 21-22 presents New Jerusalem replacing the old universe and shows a vision about eternal life as an uninterrupted, loving fellowship with God.

The First Vision

REVELATION 1

Revelation 1:1 presents John's message as the revelation or unfolding that God gave to Jesus to show Him what "must soon take place".

This verse is loaded with meaning, and it outlines the general tense of the book. It is the unfolding of what God has already planned but what has been now revealed to men. What is prophecy to us is knowledge to God. But it "must soon take place". This means that Revelation is not just a book about a distant, apocalyptic future. It means that when we try to understand it, we must begin from John and not from our present time. A great mistake many interpreters make is to ignore the little cues that John has placed around Revelation. Because of that, many evangelical interpreters will time nearly all the book's events, apart from the letter to the seven churches, to take place in one end-time generation.

But Revelation is not just about an end of the world at some point in future. It does not give us the freedom to speculate about its contents as some last-minute events on the final page of world history. Like the rest of the Bible prophecy, Revelation is a symbolic book, yet it is firmly rooted in historical time, and our interpretation of it must be firmly anchored in that historical time. If some of the events prophesied in the book will "soon take place" in John's time, there is a high probability that they have already become history in our time. From our vantage point, they have become fulfilled prophecies.

When a prophecy is fulfilled, it becomes *history*. It does not remain a prophecy forever. Hence when we read Revelation, we must remain open to the idea that some of it might today be history.

UNDERSTANDING REVELATION

I would suggest that what is prophesied has as much to do with *why* it will happen than *what* will happen. The prophecies in Revelation are not simply predictive but also explanatory. The past, present and future find their meaning in God.

This meaningfulness of time because God defines its significance needs to be separated from predeterminism. Not everything that happens in the world has been purposed by God, but it has *meaning* because of Him.

God's knowledge—or from our perspective, His foreknowledge—does not imply His acceptance of everything that will happen. God will never *approve* the persecution and murdering of His saints, even when He allows it to happen. But this persecution will have eternal consequences; it will not remain unaccounted for.

But whether God approves everything that will happen or not, He will work out His will through any scenario or circumstance. In fact, the end-time judgments are released because God has accomplished His will, but He will judge what has taken place in the meantime.

Revelation is the unfolding of *all time*—the past, present and future—from God's perspective.

No matter how evil and horrendous the events described in Revelation, it remains focused on God's action. The other actors described, such as the devil, might have their own plans, but it is God who will have His way in the end.

In *verse 1*, God gives this revelation to Jesus. At this point, it might seem that Revelation is describing Jesus as somewhat lower than God, as His messenger. But as we read further, we will discover that Revelation in fact presents a clear teaching about the Trinity. But certainly, this revelation would have been something that Jesus when walking on earth in flesh would probably not have known. He would have known glimpses of it, as His prophecies recorded in the Gospels demonstrate. But we will discover that this giving of revelation has as much to do with the authority to deliver it on earth and in heaven than with the knowledge about it.

In the chain of revelation-giving, God gives the revelation to Jesus, who then gives it to one of His angels, who gives it to John. This might suggest some spiritual hierarchy, with God on the throne being the

REVELATION 1

highest, Jesus and the angels in the middle and John the lowest, but that is not exactly the case, as will soon become clear.

Unless you believe that Revelation is a genuine revelation, you must take it as a false prophecy. Many seem to read it merely as a literary work, as if John had composed yet another apocalyptical book for the fiction market of speculative books. They give it some merit, yet this merit does not amount to giving it the status of divine revelation, but merely a status as a work of subjective prophetic imagination.

There is much to be said about the literary merits of Revelation. It has been constructed carefully and painstakingly, and the complex referencing to the Old Testament prophets and the consistency of it all is nothing but astounding.

But to read Revelation only as a narrative created by a fertile prophetic imagination would miss the whole point of it. We can analyse the narrative conventions in Revelation, but we must remember that narrative theory has been developed mainly in the sphere of fiction. Comparing Revelation with other apocalyptic books of the time from the perspective of genre theory misses the whole point of apocalyptic books. No matter how they have been composed, their main purpose was to predict the future. Their writers might have been false or true prophets, but they presented themselves as prophets. They were written to be taken seriously as prophecies, and that is how we should approach them.

Many writers today write speculative books about future events. Many seem to perceive Revelation as such. But by starting with the words that this is the revelation of Jesus Christ, the author objects most strongly against seeing this book as some sort of speculation. As far as John is concerned, this is not a work of poetry or imagination. There might be a lot of symbolism in it, but it all points to reality—both visible and invisible.

And this is not a revelation that John received from God, from Jesus, or even from an angel. This is a revelation that Jesus received from the Father seated on the throne.

But how did Jesus receive this revelation? *Revelation 5:6-7* says:

> And I looked, and behold, in the midst of the throne and of the four living creatures, and in the midst of the elders, stood

UNDERSTANDING REVELATION

a Lamb as though it had been slain, having seven horns and seven eyes, which are the seven Spirits of God sent out into all the earth. Then He came and took the scroll out of the right hand of Him who sat on the throne.

This suggests that this revelation is something that Jesus has received through His triumph on the cross. This is not some revelation that God has already known and has now been disclosed to Jesus. The Son of God is not inferior to God who sits on the throne, as the Son of God also has the seven spirits of God, hence He shares the divinity of God. So, this revelation is not something that God has kept away from Jesus, as if He had inferior knowledge. This is not revelation as knowledge (*gnosis*) but revelation as authority. Jesus is entitled to release it in heaven and earth because He has triumphed.

Revelation is the unfolding of God's plan through Jesus Christ because He has been given the authority to make this plan unfold.

As someone who has a prophetic ministry, this speaks to a misunderstanding that we often have about the nature of prophecy. We often see it as an insight about what God will do—as foreknowledge. If we would only receive that insight, we would know what God will do, we think. In one sense, this is right. But the foreknowledge we receive from God can never be separated from His victory. Jesus's victory on the cross entitles Him to release a new sequence of events, which will culminate in the separation between the righteous and the unrighteous in the end of time, as prophesied in Revelation.

In many ways, the Old Testament prophets had already declared much of what God will do. But now the Church, rather than Israel, has taken the central place as God's main agent on earth. But Israel has not been forgotten. Her blessings and promises have not ceased. God is faithful to His promises, and Revelation explains how both Israel and the Church remain as part of God's plan.

Far from being the book of curses many see Revelation to be, it reveals what entitles Jesus to release God's blessings on the Church. Revelation is not a book about the wrath of God but about the salvation from the wrath of God. The world is already under the wrath of God, but Revelation reveals the way out from under this wrath.

REVELATION 1

At the heart of the book is not as much revelation as the authority to reveal the revelation, which will inevitably also release the events described in it. But what is being revealed is also the interplay between God, humanity, and the works of darkness, not just the work of God. God's actions lead to reactions from the devil. But God has already anticipated those reactions.

And as much Revelation is a revelation of the Christ, it is also a revelation about the Christ.

As I have already said, many scholars today see Revelation merely as some sort of spiritual encouragement created in the fertile imagination of John of Patmos who, far from being an apostle of Jesus, was some local prophet in Asia Minor.

The reformer Martin Luther wanted to remove Revelation from the German Bible, along with the letter to the Hebrews and by James and Jude, mainly as, in his view, they did not fit well with his grace-alone doctrine. That was until he found out that he could use Revelation as a weapon against the Pope!

But although this is a revelation by Jesus, it must be a revelation in response to John's prayers that would have been prayed over many decades.

By this time, John was the last of the twelve foundational apostles alive. Peter had been martyred. Even Paul had been martyred. After the apostles had been killed, many false doctrines had materialised, as Christianity no more had its birth leaders and was drifting towards paganism. New, loud voices were preaching another gospel, and it might have looked to John that he had wasted his years toiling with no major impact.

In Jerusalem, John had known the High Priest, and it is likely that he came from a priestly family. By the time Revelation had been written, the Second Temple in Jerusalem already lay in ruins, and John had left the formerly protective confines of Judea, where the full onslaught of the surrounding pagan culture had been curtailed by the sheer force of Jewish exceptionalism.

Now he resided in the land of other gods, where the other gods claimed total domination, which was attested by the whole society, from architecture to daily life.

UNDERSTANDING REVELATION

Paul had been raised in Tarsus, a pagan city with a Jewish presence, and he had got used to paganism from birth. He could travel these lands easily, not least as he was a Roman citizen. But John was a Jew who was born and raised in the Jewish heartland.

To understand Revelation fully, we must imagine an entirely different visual landscape than today. It had an absolute pagan visual domination. This was not the world of today but the pre-Christian world where no Christian visual language existed. To begin imagining it, we would have to replace every church building with a pagan temple.

In Jerusalem and Judea there had been signs of paganism, but they could mostly have been avoided, and the temple for Yahweh had dominated the visual landscape. But in Asia Minor, Greek and Roman gods dominated the visual world.

In the Greco-Roman cities, the Jewish prophet could have escaped these visual signs of paganism only to a synagogue, but after the destruction of Jerusalem, the Jews had become even more suspicious of Jesus's followers, especially as they had not stood with them in fight against Rome. It would take two centuries before Christianity would begin to develop a visual culture, and it would be largely borrowed from paganism. Right now, the only visual symbol Christians had was a fish, as the cross had not yet developed into the prevalent Christian symbol. It is difficult for us to imagine this kind of world with no visual reference points to Christianity at all.

It is no wonder that John would have escaped this visual world to the internal world of prayer and the Jewish Scriptures. After all, he now lived in the world that was filled with idolatrous images.

Verse 3 says:

> Blessed is the one reads aloud the words of the prophecy, and blessed are those who hear and hear and who keep what is written in it; for the time is near.

This prophecy is not just for reading and hearing, but also for keeping. Responding to it demands action. But what kind of action? Revelation does have an ethical and moral dimension, but at the heart of it is a call to radical obedience, even to the point of martyrdom. So, this

REVELATION 1

spiritual action cannot properly be defined as moral or ethical action, as if we were talking in terms of some moral philosophy.

But what time is near? This must mean that at least some of the prophecies in the book are about to be fulfilled. The great unfolding of God's plan is beginning.

Verse 4 addresses the seven churches located in Asia Minor, which is the area of the modern-day Turkey. John sends peace to them from the One who is, who was and who is to come, from the seven spirits that are before God's throne, and from Jesus Christ, the faithful witness, the firstborn from the dead, and the ruler over the kings of the earth.

Often, we hear that the concept of the Trinity is not in the Bible but invented centuries later. But here we can see a clear Trinitarian formulation, although in a symbolic form. There is the One who is, who was and who is to come. This refers to God on the throne, but it could also refer to Jesus. The seven spirits refer to God on the throne, but also to the Holy Spirit and to Jesus, as the seven spirits are a clear reference to *Isaiah 11:2-3* and the seven qualities of God. John will be building and refining his Trinitarian theology through the pages of Revelation.

As I have mentioned before, Revelation should be read as a hypertext with links to the Old Testament prophecies, so that we will jump back and forth whenever we need more clarity.

Isaiah 11 contains a messianic prophecy about a rod from the stem of Jesse. This chapter is our only reference in the Bible—outside Revelation—to the seven spirits of God. Hence it must be our primary reference point in understanding what the seven spirits of God are. Isaiah foretells that the Messiah will have the seven spirits of God. Before that, in *Isaiah 9:1-7,* the prophet has already told us that the Messiah who will be born as a child will be called "Wonderful, Counselor, Mighty God, Everlasting Father, Prince of Peace." So, although Revelation is referring to Jesus as the "faithful witness", it also tells that if you look deeper, you will find out from Isaiah's prophecy that He is the Messiah, and that this Messiah is God Himself.

But He is also the faithful witness, and anyone facing violence and persecution, even until martyrdom, can draw strength from the fact that the testimony of Jesus had to withstand even death on the cross. What we must withstand in life God Himself has already withstood in

UNDERSTANDING REVELATION

flesh. And now He is the witness about the eternal world and eternal life that we are unable to see with our natural eyes.

Jesus, accounted by the same John in *John 3:12-13*, says:

> If I have told you about earthly things and you do not believe, how can you believe if I tell you about heavenly things? No one has ascended into heaven except the one who descended from heaven, the Son of Man.

And now He has returned to John to tell him about these heavenly things in detail.

The One who is on the throne and Jesus are united by the seven spirits, which are distinct from the One who is on the throne, and yet they are God's Spirit.

Revelation is full of symbolic numbers, and here the seven spirits refer to the perfection and completeness of God's Spirit, as in *Isaiah 11*. There are no seven holy spirits but One Perfect Spirit of God.

In *Revelation 1:10*, John was "in the Spirit", so the beginning of the book outlines beautifully and poetically the way the triune God works in the world and in our lives. His love for us is so great that even when the Father stays on the throne, He has come to us both as the Son and the Spirit.

Through the Son and the Spirit, God has reached out to humanity with all of Himself whilst remaining on the throne. There is no more of Him God could give to us whilst we are still on earth.

What John is telling through his hyperlinks to the Old Testament prophecy is that Jesus came from heaven and that the messianic prophecies have been fulfilled in Him.

Clearly John expects many of the readers to know the Jewish Bible, and there would have been many Christian Jews in most Christian communities in Asia Minor. So, when he links Jesus in Revelation with *Isaiah 11*, he would have expected many of the readers to be able to make that connection. But because we do not know the Old Testament as well as the Jews, most of these references are lost to even many Bible scholars, especially if their sole focus of research is the New Testament.

REVELATION 1

Prophecy About the End-Time Israel

Also, this reference to the seven spirits of God in *verse 4* takes us to the second return of Jews from the exile prophesied in *Isaiah 11*. This second return was fulfilled in 1948 with the birth of the modern Israel. After messianic prophecies about Jesus, *Isaiah 11* continues to predict how the modern Israel will dominate the Middle East until the Kingdom of Peace under the rule of the Messiah.

Isaiah 11:14 says,

> But they shall fly down upon the shoulder of the Philistines toward the west; together they shall plunder the people of the East; they shall lay their hand on Edom and Moab; and the people of Ammon shall obey them.

The text of Revelation is arranged in such a way that the reader is supposed to follow these references to the Old Testament, which will then give the reader a fuller understanding of both Revelation and the Old Testament prophecy.

The present-day Israel inhabits nearly half of the biblical Edom. This Isaiah's prophecy referenced to in *Revelation 1* to provide a chronological sequence of Israel's future gives an accurate size of the end-time Israel.

It is fascinating that the beginning of the book that will later recount the destruction of the Second Temple in AD 70 predicts the birth of the end-time Israel through referencing the Old Testament. Many of the book's readers were still struggling to cope with the destruction of the Second Temple in Jerusalem. It had stood for hundreds of years, but now nothing was left of it, and its treasures had been carried to Rome as a booty. John's readers were fully aware that Jerusalem had been destroyed; this was the most catastrophic event in the history of the Jewish nation since the exile to Babylon. What the Jewish Christians lacked was hope that Israel could ever rise again.

What becomes clear is that the modern Israel has nothing to fear: God will be her protector. No matter how we see the Middle East politically, this is God's promise. Paradoxically, many Christians who profess to believe in Bible prophecy behave and speak as if Israel's survival depended on us. It does not. Already, in *verse 4* of the first

UNDERSTANDING REVELATION

chapter of Revelation John is declaring the end-time return of the Jews back to Israel. But you will grasp that only if you know the writings of the Old Testament prophets intimately.

There are different sizes given to Israel in the Bible, and it is a mistake to apply the largest version to every time of Israel's existence, including today.

John is explaining the prophecies of Isaiah by reminding that although the Second Temple and much of Jerusalem had been destroyed in his time, the Jews would one day return.

The relationship between the southwestern Jordan and Palestine is an interesting one, as it reflects this domination. I feel deep sympathy with the Palestinians, not least as our ministry has worked for many years with the Arabs and other groups in the Middle East. But according to the Bible, the end-time Israel will be in a militarily dominating position. Yet, *Isaiah 11* does not predict the nearly limitless Israel that some Zionistic Christians refer to justify anything the state of Israel will ever set out to do. This is a limited Israel but with a clear dominating position over the region.

Hence, from the beginning of Revelation, it is made clear that you need to understand the Old Testament prophecies to understand Revelation, and that Revelation also explains Old Testament prophecies. In fact, Revelation is a continuation of the Old Testament prophetic books, and it is in a continual conversation with them. To John, the Old Testament prophets are his contemporaries, as they all speak from the perspective of eternity.

We can see how densely packed Revelation is with message and meaning. We have only read a few verses, and we have already encountered a clear formulation of the triune God and a prophecy about the end-time Israel.

Verses 5-6 about us being kings and priests, because He has washed us from our sins in His own blood, have a clear reference point in *Psalm 110*, which prophesies that the Messiah will be King but also Priest, and then extends these offices to us. But the fulfilment of this promise has a clear anchor point in the end-times: according to *Psalm 110:5*, it is "in the day of His wrath", when He shall judge the nations. But it is the rule of the Messiah that will bring the fulfilment of all God's promises to Israel. Only the Messiah can bring Israel's fullness.

REVELATION 1

So, the simple device of placing a reference to *Isaiah 11* before a reference to *Psalm 110* gives us an end-time chronology linked to the modern Israel.

The events will unfold sequentially, and waiting for things to happen in the wrong order is a mistake.

Verse 7 says:

> Behold, He is coming with clouds, and every eye will see Him, even they who pierced Him. And all the tribes of the earth will mourn because of Him. Even so, Amen.

The Old Testament reference point for this prophecy can be found in *Zechariah 12:10*, which predicts the end-time repentance of Israel. Earlier, Revelation has referred to Isaiah's prophecy about Israel that would dominate the region after a remnant would return in the end-times. Now, Revelation hyperlinks us to Israel that will be attacked by the nations, before the eyes of Israel will finally be opened to understand whom they have pierced.

We can see how the arrangement of the Old Testament references becomes a prophetic interpretation of Old Testament prophecy.

So, according to this end-time chronology, hidden in plain sight in the beginning of Revelation, the full return of Israel to God is one of the final acts and will coincide with the day of God's wrath. Again. we must read around the exact reference point in the Old Testtament to gain full understanding.

"All the nations are gathered against it", *Zechariah 12:3* says. This is a reference to an end-time battle against Israel. Often, our interpretation of Bible prophecy can be distorted by whatever the state of international politics happens to be in our time. But what John appears to be saying is that after the return of the Jews to Israel for the second time, Israel will dominate the region, until all the nations will gather against it.

But whereas in *Zechariah 12* only Israel will mourn for the pierced one, in *Revelation 1* the whole earth is mourning because of Him. But this is also a clear reference to Jesus returning both to the living and the dead. This raises the question in which manner Jesus will return the second time—does Jesus "return" to us the second time when we die, or is there a day of one cosmic return? Do the dead sleep, and are they raised on the final day, or do they rise straight after they die?

As we will see shortly, John is writing to congregations that would have been familiar with the teachings of the apostle Paul. And Paul writes in *1 Thessalonians 4:14-17*:

> For if we believe that Jesus died and rose again, even so God will bring with Him those who sleep in Jesus. For this we say to you by the word of the Lord, that we who are alive *and* remain until the coming of the Lord will by no means precede those who are asleep. For the Lord Himself will descend from heaven with a shout, with the voice of an archangel, and with the trumpet of God. And the dead in Christ will rise first. Then we who are alive *and* remain shall be caught up together with them in the clouds to meet the Lord in the air. And thus we shall always be with the Lord.

Paul says that the dead in Christ will rise first. And the ones who are alive shall be caught up with them in the clouds.

It appears that Paul clearly believes in the final day of resurrection, but things might not be as straightforward as they seem, as Paul does not give us the time difference between the raising of those who have died and those who will be on earth in the return of Jesus. We will see later in Revelation how John believes that those who have died in Christ are already in heaven. This will have major implications on how we interpret his account of the Millennial Kingdom.

If we let John interpret Paul, that could mean that there can be a significant time difference between the raising of those already dead and whichever generation will witness the return of Jesus. Neither does Paul state that meeting with the Lord would be an event noticed by the whole world, so that leaves many options open.

Focal Shift from Israel to the Church

Revelation 1 begins to introduce the fundamental focal shifts from Israel to the whole world and from Israel to the Church. The Church is now at the heart of God's plan. At the centre of Revelation is the planting of the mustard seed, the Church, her growth, and her eventual

REVELATION 1

position as a large tree, where the birds will make their nests, as Jesus tells us in *Matthew 13:31–32*.

Verse 8 says:

> "I am the Alpha and the Omega, *the* Beginning and *the* End," says the Lord, "who is and who was and who is to come, the Almighty."

Revelation explains the beginning and the ending, and what *is*. God is not bound by our understanding of time, and, because of this, we should be open to the possibility that Revelation does not only reveal the future but also the past—and the present moment in time of writing. Through Revelation runs not just future prediction but also unfolding of how things really are. And not just that; Revelation also reveals to us what *happened*. But this formulation is not John's invention, for *Isaiah 41:4* says, "I, the Lord, am first; and will be with the last." The Alpha and Omega is a Greek translation of the formulation first offered to us by Isaiah, which presents the Almighty God to us as the beginner and ender of all things. We are again reminded of the intimate relationship between the Old Testament prophets and Revelation.

God is almighty now and in future, as He has been in the past, and according to *Isaiah 41:26*, He declares "from the beginning, so that we might know". Not only will He act, but He will also declare what He will do in advance.

Deuteronomy 29:29 says something fascinating about the nature of revelation:

> The secret things belong to the Lord our God, but the revealed things belong to us and to our children forever, to observe all the words of this law.

There is finality and extreme power to God's revelation. When He finally reveals it to us, it becomes fixed and belongs to us forever. That is why Revelation is the "revelation of Jesus Christ"; it is He who has acquired this revelation for us through His triumph on the cross. The cost of this revelation has been paid with His blood.

By now it should be clear that John is not presenting this book as an allegory or solely as an interpretation of the current situation

UNDERSTANDING REVELATION

of his time, but that he is also declaring things that will happen in future. But this reference of God being in the past, present and future should also tell us that not everything in the book might be predictive. Instead, there is a possibility that John's visions might also be looking backwards to explain what has already taken place.

Verse 9 says:

> I, John, your brother who share with you in Jesus the persecution and the kingdom and the patient endurance, was on the island called Patmos because of the word of God and the testimony of Jesus.

A loud voice, "as of a trumpet", tells him that He is "the Alpha and the Omega", also "the First and Last", and asks him to write a book and send it to the seven churches in Asia: Ephesus, Smyrna, Pergamum, Thyatira, Sardis, Philadelphia, and Laodicea.

Patmos is an island on the Turkish coastline not so far from the seven churches John was writing to, with Ephesus being the nearest. If the book was delivered to churches whilst John still resided in Patmos, Ephesus would have been the first church to receive it. Smyrna is located north of Ephesus, and the practical order for the letter to travel would have been from Ephesus to Smyrna, and then further north to Pergamum, after which it would have travelled southeast and finally reached Laodicea in the exact order mentioned in the book.

So, there is a clear geographical logic to the order the cities are introduced.

Eusebius of Caesaria, who became the bishop of Caesarea Maritima around AD 314, wrote the first chronological church history. Often, theologians discount the early church history as inaccurate, but even if Eusebius got many facts wrong, there is no reason to suspect that everything he wrote was wrong. And, according to his *The Church History* (Book 3, Ch. 4), Paul's associate Timothy was the first bishop of the church in Ephesus.

Often, theologians seem to be more suspicious of historical documents linked to the Church than historians, perhaps because they compare them to the Word of God, which used to be, according to

REVELATION 1

theologians, infallible. But often historians, who are used to perceiving historical documents as fallible, tend to give them more credence, as their expectation never was infallibility.

According to Eusebius, John was condemned to live on the island of Patmos after Domitian gained power as emperor (Book 3, Ch. 18), and he could return from the island only after the death of Domitian. John settled in Ephesus, staying there until the rule of Emperor Trajan. (Book 3, Ch. 20, Ch. 23). Domitian was the Roman emperor between AD 81 and AD 96. He was the younger brother of Titus and the son of Vespasian, who both preceded him on the throne, and the third and last member of the Flavian dynasty.

Also, Irenaeus says that Revelation "was seen no very long time since, but almost in our day, towards the end of Domitian's reign." (*Against Heresies* 5.30.3)

If we believe the tradition passed down to us by Eusebius, it means that Revelation was written somewhere between AD 81 and AD 96, whilst John was in exile in Patmos. There are many alternative dates offered, though, and many good reasons can be found within the book to assume that at least some of it might have been revealed to John during the reign of Emperor Vespasian.

It might appear that John saw all of Revelation in one lengthy revelation, but this is unlikely. In fact, it is more likely that John would have seen a series of revelations not necessarily in the order listed in the book and with lengthy times of prayer and reflection in between.

Also, there might have been quite a lengthy time between the initial writing of Revelation and when it was distributed beyond the seven churches. After all, in comparison to Paul's letters, this book is not easy to comprehend, although even Peter in *2 Peter 3:15* writes that many found Paul's letters too hard to understand. So, if you find Paul's letters difficult to understand, you will probably find Revelation impossible to understand!

And just because John addresses the seven churches, most of which he would have been familiar with, it does not mean that the letter would have been delivered to them immediately after he received this part of Revelation. Anyone working with lengthy prophecies and with sharing them would have been spending plenty of time to ensure that he would get every word right when writing them down. And even when Revelation is a series of visions, it still has signs of masterful composition. It bears the marks of prayerful editing.

John writes as a companion to the tribulation, indicating that he had also suffered from persecution.

In the New Testament era Ephesus was the fourth largest city in the world—after Rome, Alexandria, and Antioch—with the population of about 250,000. Today, the magnitude of this city is lost to many Bible readers, as there is not much left of the ancient Ephesus.

Both Acts and Paul's letters attest that Paul sought to establish churches in large cities, such as Galatia, Thessalonica, Corinth, and Ephesus, making them mission centres. Ignatius, the first-century Christian writer and bishop, refers to churches planted from Ephesus. It was the principal centre from which missions came forth to plant the other churches in Asia Minor. (Dunn 2009, 555-557)

It is quite possible that the church of Ephesus was the mother church of all these other churches mentioned in Revelation. So, John might not be referring to seven churches but to one church that started six other churches. In any case, these seven churches were by no means the only churches in Asia Minor at this time, so these churches must have been chosen deliberately.

We can see traces of Ephesus' influence in the New Testament. It is the third most mentioned city in the New Testament, after Jerusalem and Nazareth. In fact, for hundreds of years, before the rise of Rome as the centre of the Western Christendom, Ephesus was the main centre of the Church. For example, the Council of Ephesus took place in the city in AD 431, and the previous two ecumenical councils also took place in this city in the territory of the modern-day Turkey.

Before Rome, there was Ephesus. And what happened in Ephesus would in many ways define the Church until the Reformation, so it is not a coincidence that the first church addressed by Jesus was Ephesus.

High Priest in the Temple

When John turns to see who is speaking, he sees seven golden lampstands, and in their midst "one like the Son of Man", who is also the "First and the Last". That Jesus is God could not be made any clearer.

REVELATION 1

Verses 14-15 say that the Son of Man is:

> Clothed with a garment down to the feet and girded about the chest with a golden band. His head and hair *were* white like wool, as white as snow, and His eyes like a flame of fire; His feet *were* like fine brass, as if refined in a furnace, and His voice as the sound of many waters; He had in His right hand seven stars, out of His mouth went a sharp two-edged sword, and His countenance *was* like the sun shining in its strength.

The Son of Man is God but also the High Priest. He lives although He was dead, and He now has the keys of Hades and Death.

According to *John 18:15*, the apostle John knew the High Priest Caiaphas, who condemned Jesus to death in the hands of the Romans. This implies that John would have come from a family of priests. He would probably have been a Levite.

In *The Church History*, Eusebius quotes Polycrates of Ephesus who lived around AD 130-196, according to whom John was "both a witness and a teacher, who reclined upon the bosom of the Lord, and, being a priest, wore the sacerdotal plate." (Book III, Ch. 31)

It is impossible to assess the historicity of the claim about John wearing a physical priestly breastplate, but it seems sensible to assume that John would have been a priest, especially as that is consistent with the Gospel of John and the fact that John seems to have known the High Priest. And it would have taken someone with detailed knowledge of the Jewish Scriptures to write Revelation.

Here John paints a picture of the High Priest in the Temple. The number of the seven lampstands is identical to Menorah in the Jewish Temple, but unlike with Menorah, these seven lampstands are separate.

The meaning of this is clear: there is a new temple, and it incorporates the Church. It is not my intention to promote replacement theology, but it is evident that in John and Paul's thinking the Church has replaced Israel as the main agent of God in the world. It is the Church rather than Israel carrying God's Spirit.

Verse 19 says: "Now write what you have seen, what is, and what is to take place after this." It is evident that some of the events John will be writing about had already taken place.

UNDERSTANDING REVELATION

The destruction of the Second Temple in AD 70 is one of the most catastrophic events in the Jewish history. According to Josephus, a Jewish historian and former general with intimate knowledge of the First Jewish-Roman War (AD 66-73), around one million people, mostly Jews, were killed during the siege. Nearly hundred thousand were captured, and many were forced to become gladiators and perish on the arena.

The overarching storyline of Revelation is the destiny of the temple. It accounts the destruction of the Second Temple, but it presents the Church as the new temple on earth, and heaven as the final temple of God, or rather, God Himself as the final temple in heaven. Therefore, it is a fitting finale to the Bible.

Genesis 1-2 says that we are images of God—the connecting points between earth and God. Genesis does not tell that the Spirit of God resided in man in Paradise, but only that man had access to God's presence, or rather that God would visit man whenever He wished. After the Fall, it is Moses who introduced the temple on earth as an external tabernacle, but it was an external place with very limited access to God's presence. The coming of Jesus brought the destruction of the external temple, but the temple moved into us. We are no more just images of God, reflecting His glory, but His glory now resides within us. But in this bodily temple we can experience the presence of God only in a limited way, whereas in New Jerusalem we will be able to experience His presence with no limitation.

In the vision, the Son of Man is dressed like the High Priest, and He is looking after the candle stands, ensuring that their fire will continue to burn.

Against the Worship of Angels
Revelation 1:20 says:

> As for the mystery of the seven stars that you saw in my right hand, and the seven golden lampstands: the seven stars are the angels of the seven churches, and the seven lampstands are the seven churches.

REVELATION 1

The Son of Man holds the seven stars in His hand. This indicates that the angelic forces represented by the stars are commanded by the Son of Man. They are not independent agents, but they will do only what the Son of Man will command them to do. They are not our servants but God's servants, fully obedient to Him.

Paul writes in *Colossians 2:18-19:*

> Do not let anyone disqualify you, insisting on self-abasement and worship of angels, dwelling on visions, puffed up without cause by a human way of thinking, and not holding fast to the head, from whom the whole body, nourished and held together by its ligaments and sinews, grows with a growth that is from God.

Colossae was located only ten miles from Laodicea, and this problem with angel worship in churches was not unique to this city.

Horsley and Luxford present a fascinating study of the epigraphic evidence of pagan angels in Roman Asia Minor. Angels have widely been assumed to come to pagan thinking from Judaism at later date, but their research shows that pagans might have believed in angels a lot longer than thought. For example, there are inscriptions in Roman Asia Minor where angels are subject to Zeus. Also, there are angels that appear as Apollo's agents in dispensing justice. (Horsley and Luxford 2016, 153, 157) These inscriptions were carved around the time of John and Paul.

In Lykia, there is an inscription from the third century that can be translated as "This is God, and we *angeloi* [angels] are a small portion of God." (ibid., 159)

According to Horsey and Luxford (ibid., 177-178), the dichotomy between good and bad angels that developed in Judaism is lacking in the pagan descriptions of angels, perhaps because the pagan system was not monotheistic. There have been suggestions that the angels in Roman Asia Minor had a Persian origin. But perhaps they had multiple origins, and there was no consistent belief system around them.

But we can now understand how it would have been easy for the Greeks coming from a polytheistic religious system to attribute divinity to angels after they converted to Christianity. After all, in the pagan system, the angels were a portion of God, and not that dissimilar from the Greek gods. For them, angels provided a bridge between Christianity and paganism, and talking about angels to pagans would have been a lot less offensive than talking about the crucified Christ.

So, when Paul writes about wrestling against evil principalities and powers in the heavenly realms in *Ephesians 6:12*, he is perhaps also seeking to debunk an idea that somehow these forces represented by Greek and Roman gods could have been in the service of God. Instead, Paul says that they represent a separate spiritual system that is hostile to God.

Here John presents in a visual way the supremacy of Christ over the unfallen angels that serve Him. Jesus is almighty, and the mighty angels are mere tools in his hand. They are directed by Jesus's hand. They are God's messengers.

This is also a vision about Jesus as the King of Kings, as it resembles a popular Roman coin. An *aureus*—a Roman gold coin valued at 25 silver denarii—of the empress Domitia, the wife of Emperor Domitian, depicts the deified infant son of the emperor seated on the globe and stretching his hands to seven stars (Hemer 2001, 4).

Whereas the Roman coin depicted the son of the emperor reaching out to the Roman gods and being lower than the stars, Revelation portrays Jesus as the Lord over the seven stars, which in this description are angels. This reference to angels as stars will reappear in *Revelation 12:4*, where one third of the stars follow the dragon. Through this imagery John depicts the gods that the son of the emperor worships as nothing more than fallen stars—demons.

We can begin to see the assault on the Roman belief system and gods, including the deified emperor, which permeates large parts of Revelation, including John's description of the beast.

But the most important reference point is not a Roman coin but *Habakkuk 3:3-5*:

> God came from Teman, the Holy One from Mount Paran. Selah. His glory covered the heavens, and the earth was full of his praise. The brightness was like the sun; rays came forth from his hand, where his power lay hidden. Before him went pestilence, and plague followed close behind.

REVELATION 1

Like the bright stars, rays were flashing from His hand. Both Habakkuk and Revelation present Jesus as God, the Holy One, who will also bring pestilence. Ultimately, all the pestilences that will follow in Revelation are His judgment. We can see how skilfully Revelation weaves together the biblical imagery with the situation that the Christians found themselves in the Roman Empire. But Habakkuk's text itself is a reference to Moses' final blessing of Israel in *Deuteronomy 33:1-2*:

> This is the blessing with which Moses, the man of God, blessed the Israelites before his death. He said: "The Lord came from Sinai, and dawned from Seir upon us; he shone forth from Mount Paran. With him were myriads of holy ones; at his right, a host of his own."

This blessing comes straight after the Song of Moses in Deuteronomy; the Song of Moses is referred to later in Revelation. We begin to see how Revelation is making continual references to the Law and the Prophets: *the two witnesses*.

By using symbolic language that refers to the Old Testament texts, Revelation claims that both the Law and the Prophets testify that Jesus is God. Later in Revelation, we will reencounter these two witnesses. Then, they will testify against Jerusalem.

REVELATION 2

Ephesus

Revelation 2 begins with Jesus addressing the church in Ephesus, or rather the angel of Ephesus. Some commentators understand the angels of the seven churches to be the elders of the seven churches, but that is a misinterpretation, as all this is to underline that the angels are subject to Jesus.

Jesus is speaking to one of the stars in His hand—the angel of Ephesus. This means that the angels themselves are unable to produce any revelation. But they are directed by Jesus's hand. In Revelation, the angels that do not follow the orders of Jesus are in rebellion against Him together with Satan.

In *Revelation 2:1,* Jesus walks amongst the seven golden lampstands. This means that these seven churches are each a separate church with different lives and trajectories, yet they all are in the temple of the Lord and in His presence. The Menorah of Israel, one lampstand with seven candles, can no more be seen.

Today, the Menorah, as portrayed on the Arch of Titus in Rome, which depicts the destruction of Jerusalem by Titus, together with two olive branches, is the symbol of the modern state of Israel. The Menorah with two olive branches is also the vision the prophet saw in *Zechariah 4* regarding the rebuilding of the temple after the return from the exile in Babylon.

The absence of the Jewish Menorah in John's vision about the temple means that the Second Temple has already been destroyed. This has been the judgment of God on Israel and Jerusalem. The Menorah of Israel has now been replaced in the temple of God by the

UNDERSTANDING REVELATION

Church, represented by the seven separate candles. The seven churches symbolise the fullness of the Church, the Church in her totality. In some ways, the seven churches must be representative of all churches, even when Jesus is talking to the specific situations of these seven churches at the time of John receiving the revelation.

Revelation 2:2 says:

> I know that you cannot tolerate evildoers; you have tested those who claim to be apostles but are not, and have found them to be false.

It seems reasonable to trust the church tradition about John, the apostle and Jesus's disciple, leading the church in Ephesus sometime after Paul's martyrdom. It seems that after Paul's departure false apostles had arrived in Ephesus, either before or after John himself had been there. And it appears that the Christians in Ephesus had tested these apostles and found them to be liars.

Paul prophesied about these wolf-like apostles when he said farewell to the Christians in Ephesus. Paul says in *Acts 20:29-31*:

> I know that after I have gone, savage wolves will come in among you, not sparing the flock. Some even from your own group will come distorting the truth in order to entice the disciples to follow them. Therefore be alert, remembering that for three years I did not cease night or day to warn everyone with tears.

There is a remarkable consistency between Revelation, Acts and Paul's teaching. When it comes to the literary genre, they are stylistically different, but theologically they are fully consistent with each other.

In *Revelation 2:4*, Jesus reprimands the church in Ephesus for forsaking their first love. This reprimand has been understood in different ways, but most have interpreted it as command to fall in love with Jesus again.

But because of the later historical development in the Ephesian church, this reprimand is probably more precise than a general admonition. If we accept Revelation as prophecy, then we must consider that it might be referring to a syncretistic development in

REVELATION 2

Ephesus that would take some centuries to develop fully but would shape the global Church until the Reformation and is continuing to affect many branches of the Church today.

In times of Paul and John, Ephesus and the goddess Artemis were inseparable, with Artemis Ephesia being the personification of the whole city (Strelan 2014, 46). Ephesus did eventually become an important Christian city, but for centuries, the church there existed in the shadow of Artemis.

By and large, in the ancient world access to the power of gods and benefactors was perceived to take place through their image. In official religion, this happened only through the official image. The wellbeing of the *polis*—a Greek city—was maintained by its citizens, and it was considered their primary duty. When citizens honoured the gods of the city, they also honoured the city. Inscriptions in the temple of Artemis indicate that the conferral and reception of citizenship were sacred acts. Apparently, priests presided at the banquets that followed the sacrifices offered by the new citizens, and, by a process of casting lots, they admitted new citizens into their respective social categories, as if they were carrying the will of the goddess. Citizens were allotted to a specific tribe and thousand. In the fourth century BC there were five Ephesian tribes, later at least eight. (ibid., 31-32, 74)

Ephesus was a city owned by Artemis and built around her. You could not be a citizen of Ephesus without worshipping Artemis; you could reside there, but the price of citizenship was the public worship of Artemis.

Acts 19:35 says:

> But when the town clerk had quieted the crowd, he said, "Citizens of Ephesus, who is there that does not know that the city of the Ephesians is the temple keeper of the great Artemis and of the statue that fell from heaven?"

The town clerk addressed the citizens specifically when he incited people against Paul, as it was their civic duty to defend Artemis.

There is a clear historical and well documented continuity between the worship of Artemis and veneration of the Virgin Mary. And this continuity was endorsed by the Council of Ephesus, a gathering of Christian bishops, in AD 431.

UNDERSTANDING REVELATION

Over the first centuries of the Church, the veneration of Mary began to increase. We can see signs of it in the *Protoevangelium of James*, written mid-second century, with this apocryphal text beginning to make a case for Mary's perpetual virginity.

There is a reference in the late fourth century to an apparition of the Virgin Mary to one Gregory the Wonderworker, with Mary appearing as bright as the sun. A papyrus fragment from the early fourth century records a prayer asking for Mary's intercession. But popular devotion to Mary did not become widespread until the latter part of the fifth century. The Catholic commentators see the increase in Mary devotion as an aftermath of the Council of Ephesus, where Mary was proclaimed to be the *Theokotos*—the God-bearer. (Carroll 1992, 4, 5, 431)

The Council of Ephesus was a gathering of Christian bishops organised by the Roman Emperor Theodosius II. It declared that Jesus was one person, and not two separate persons, and possessed both a human and divine nature. Also, Mary was declared as the one who gave birth to God.

The cult statues of both Artemis and Isis from Hellenistic times show them as holding in their hand a lighted torch, symbolising their role as moon goddess, bringer of light, and bringer of children into light. This new Mary of AD 431 was an assimilation of the goddesses Isis and Artemis into Mary—the fusing of the Great Virgin with the Universal Mother. When the bishops emerged from the church dedicated to Mary, they were escorted by women bearing lighted torches. These torches were the symbol of women that were associated with the Isis-Artemis cult. (McGuckin 2008, 13-14)

It seems that the people who received this new position of Mary most enthusiastically were the devotees of Artemis. Yet this was not some haphazard reaction to some random side effects of an outcome of a theological debate but an outcome of deliberate planning by the bishops.

The church where this Council of Ephesus gathered, dedicated to the Virgin Mary, was built within the precinct of Artemision, the temple of Artemis. This symbolised the assimilation of the attributes of Artemis in those of Mary. (Merlini 2011, 151)

REVELATION 2

It appears that in the minds of the followers of Artemis, this new confirmed position of Mary as the God-bearer was a major victory.

The link to Artemis is amplified in Revelation by the reference to the Tree of Life. A reader might assume that this is a reference to the Tree of Life in Eden mentioned in *Genesis 2*. This is true, but when it comes to Ephesus, this reference has a double meaning, as Artemis was also symbolised by a tree of life. Tree, like the bee and stag were distinctively associated with Artemis Ephesia and used in coins. (Hemer 2001, 46, 47)

Tacitus, a Roman historian, writes in his *Annals* (3.61):

> First of all came the people of Ephesus. They declared that Diana and Apollo were not born at Delos, as was the vulgar belief. They had in their own country a river Cenchrius, a grove Ortygia, where Latona, as she leaned in the pangs of labour on an olive still standing, gave birth to those two deities, whereupon the grove at the divine intimation was consecrated.

The Roman goddess Diana was identified with Artemis, and, according to the Ephesians, she was born at a grove, which was then consecrated. An image of an olive tree as a tree of life, standing in a middle of a grove, is not that dissimilar to the image of the Tree of Life in the Garden of Eden. What Revelation is saying is that rather than eating from the "tree of life" in the Artemis's grove, the Ephesians should aspire to eat from the real Tree of Life, in the Garden of Eden, as it was only God rather than Artemis who could give an eternal life.

Every Ephesian and most people in Asia Minor would have been aware of this symbolism that linked the tree of life to Artemis. This reference would not have been missed by the Ephesian Christians.

In the seventy years following Emperor Constantine's death in AD 337, seventy-six pagan sacrifices were outlawed, many pagan temples were dismantled or converted to secular use, and pagan priests ceased receiving support from the state. All pagans were barred from holding office in the state administration or the army. Death penalty for baptised Christians who lapsed into paganism was introduced. The cult of Mary emerged immediately after this transformation. (Carroll 1992, 76-77)

UNDERSTANDING REVELATION

It seems clear that the cult of Artemis was transformed into the cult of Mary as paganism went "underground" in the Roman Empire. And this process started in Ephesus, where it was impossible to be a citizen unless you worshipped Artemis. It seems evident that Christian Ephesians began to venerate Mary because she provided a convenient bridge between Christianity and paganism.

Mary is known by many different names, including the Blessed Mother, Madonna, Our Lady, Star of the Sea, Queen of Heaven, and so on. Isis was a major goddess in the ancient Egyptian religion, whose worship spread throughout the Greco-Roman world. Both Isis and Mary are depicted in art as being maternal and holding their infant deities. Artemis, on the other hand, was called the Queen of Heaven.

As the worship of pagan gods was outlawed, Mary seems to have replaced both goddesses as the Mother of God and the Queen of Heaven, and from those days onwards, and even earlier, many Christians have expressed more love to Mary than to Christ, with Mary becoming the first love in large parts of the Church, so that many Christians do not even dare to approach Jesus directly but believe that they can only do it through Mary. Paul writes in *1 Timothy 2:5*:

> For there is one God; there is also one mediator between God and humankind, Christ Jesus, himself human.

The Ephesians introduced Mary as the mediator between man and Jesus. As Timothy became the first Christian bishop of Ephesus, this message about Jesus as the only mediator between God and man would have been sent to Ephesus through many messengers, including Timothy.

The surrounding culture affects every church—our era is the era of church as a performance; in Ephesus and Asia Minor, the Early Church was surrounded by the culture of Artemis. In this light, the words of Jesus sound remarkably merciful. He is not saying that a Christian cannot respect Mary, only that He should be our first love.

Paul gives the most detailed presentation of spiritual warfare in the Bible to the Christians in Ephesus (*Ephesians 6:10-18*), whose

REVELATION 2

Artemis was the most popular deity in the whole Roman Empire. It seems that at least some of that spiritual war was lost.

In *Acts 19*, we see how Paul's ministry temporarily affected the business around Artemis, but decades later the Artemis industry still seemed to be booming. For example, around AD 162-164, a decree increased the holy days dedicated to Artemis to a whole month each year (Strelan 2014, 46). So, well over hundred years after Paul's ministry in Ephesus, the Artemis cult was still expanding, with one twelfth of the year spent celebrating her. This was bound to affect the Christians in Ephesus, who after all did rightfully hold Mary to have had a special role in salvation history.

It is not difficult to imagine how the Ephesian Christians would have discovered that portraying Mary as the Queen of Heaven and Mother of God rather than focusing on the crucified Christ might have sounded like a viable evangelistic strategy. Based on the evidence of history, it is evident that Mary became the bridge between Christianity and paganism, but this affected Christianity and not just paganism, so that rather than worshipping Christ, many Christians started to worship Mary—and through her, Artemis.

There is plenty of evidence to support this conclusion. For example, in *The Protoevangelium of James*, Mary is spinning a purple templar yarn of wool, when the archangel Gabriel appears to her and declares that she will conceive from God. Why would an apocryphal book add this detail about spinning? The reason is simple.

The virginal Artemis was known for spinning. The spindle was an attribute of Artemis who is portrayed on Corinthian vases with her priestesses holding the spinning tool. (Merlini 2011, 155) So, by putting Mary to spin the temple curtain that was torn when Jesus died, the writer of the apocryphal gospel is not just adding some drama, but clearly connecting Mary to Artemis, "the spinner of life".

If you travel in Italy today, you will encounter local Mary cults. The traditions of these cults originate from over 2,500 years ago—long before Jesus was born.

There have been many potential explanations offered regarding Jesus threatening that He would remove the lampstand unless the Ephesian Christians repented, such as the fact that eventually the church in Ephesus was eradicated by Islam, and the city itself is in ruins. But there is no great mystery to it if you know the message of the Old Testament prophets.

Zechariah 4:1-5 says:

> The angel who talked with me came again, and wakened me, as one is wakened from sleep. He said to me, "What do you see?" And I said, "I see a lampstand all of gold, with a bowl on the top of it; there are seven lamps on it, with seven lips on each of the lamps that are on the top of it. And by it there are two olive trees, one on the right of the bowl and the other on its left." I said to the angel who talked with me, "What are these, my lord?" Then the angel who talked with me answered me, "Do you not know what these are?" I said, "No, my lord."

Zechariah 4:11-14 adds:

> Then I said to him, "What are these two olive trees on the right and the left of the lampstand?" And a second time I said to him, "What are these two branches of the olive trees, which pour out the oil through the two golden pipes?" He said to me, "Do you not know what these are?" I said, "No, my lord." Then he said, "These are the two anointed ones who stand by the Lord of the whole earth."

Following the prophet Zechariah's description of the lampstands, removing a lampstand would also remove it from the pipe that pumps oil into the lamp. The Holy Spirit is no more bringing life to that church. This does not mean that individual believers do not have life, but as a body the church has ceased to have life.

Many years ago, I had a strange spiritual experience when I visited the Sistine Chapel in Rome. Surrounded by the opulence of the Vatican, the chapel seems rather ascetic, even when it has been decorated by majestic frescoes, including the Creation of Adam by Michelangelo.

As I stood there, I saw a vision. In this vision, I could see smoke coming from a fire that had once burnt there. At the time, I thought that God was telling me through the vision that fire had once burnt in this place. It appears to me that a fire had been extinguished, because there was no more oil, as the lampstand had been removed.

REVELATION 2

I have many Catholic friends, and they would be the first ones to acknowledge the shortcomings of the Vatican. And none of them venerate Mary or pray to her. Instead, the pray to Christ.

It was Ephesus that created the cult of Mary, but Rome found it useful. But we should not rush to condemn all Catholics. Jesus did not say that Christians in Ephesus should forsake all the other loves. He only said that our love for Christ should be greater than for anything else. He should be our first love. So, perhaps there is a place for honouring Mary in Christianity, but not for her to replace Jesus as the Mediator between man and God.

And nothing in the reading says that a lampstand cannot be put back. When a church returns to focusing on Jesus as the Mediator, God will deal with it as He has dealt with Israel or a prodigal son.

If you are a Protestant, you should be careful not to despise those churches that appear to venerate Mary, as many Protestant churches have also forsaken their first love—only for other reasons.

On another level, we all must inspect our hearts to know that our first love has not been replaced with another love.

Verse 6 says that the Ephesian Christians hated the works of the Nicolaitans. There is a lot of disagreement and confusion about who the Nicolaitans might have been. But the church tradition can help us here. Irenaeus writes around AD 180 in *Against Heresies* (Book I, Chapter 26):

> The Nicolaitanes are the followers of that Nicolas who was one of the seven first ordained to the *diaconate* by the *apostles*. They lead lives of unrestrained indulgence.

Irenaeus was born between AD 120 and AD 140 in Smyrna, one of the cities Revelation was addressed to. He attributes the birth of the Nicolaitan movement to Nicolas, a proselyte from Antioch, who was one of the first deacons in Jerusalem in *Acts 6:5*.

We have no reason to be over-suspicious regarding Irenaeus's knowledge of the Nicolaitans, as the distance between Ephesus and Smyrna was only about fifty miles, and the Nicolaitans operated in the whole region. What is debatable is whether it was Nicolas who started the Nicolaitan movement, or if the Nicolaitans simply appealed to him for authority. Paul writes to the Corinthians in *1 Corinthians 1:12*:

> What I mean is that each of you says, "I belong to Paul," or "I belong to Apollos," or "I belong to Cephas," or "I belong to Christ."

Christians appealed to different apostles for authority, no matter whether the apostles agreed with their appeal or not. Neither Apollos nor Cephas would have agreed to the divisions in the church of Corinth. It is easy to see how pagan converts to Christianity could have appealed to a convert, who was one of the original disciples of Jesus as their leader, when some of their practices were questioned.

This practice is relatively common even today. In my book *Supernatural Love: Releasing the Compassion of Jesus Through the Gifts of the Spirit*, I describe how many contemporary Charismatics trace down their authority to William Branham, a false prophet who operated from the 1940s to 1960s. They claim that they have inherited his mantle and hence operate in his spiritual authority.

As Irenaeus was the first church father who began to argue for apostolic succession, someone else arguing for authority based on diaconal succession was something he would remember.

Irenaeus is the nearest source that we have when it comes to understanding who the Nicolaitans might have been. It is unlikely that they would have disappeared within the few decades between the writing of Revelation and the birth of Irenaeus, but their doctrines might have evolved, as do the doctrines of those who do not base them on the Bible.

There is a high probability that Irenaeus might be correct about the origin of Nicolaitans, as Revelation distinguishes the false apostles from the Nicolaitans when addressing the Ephesians, which might imply that the Nicolaitans were not claiming apostolic but diaconal authority because of Nicolas.

Next, *Revelation 2* moves from Ephesus to Smyrna, which was located around fifty miles south of Ephesus.

REVELATION 2
Promises for the Overcomers
Before looking at Smyrna, it is useful to inspect the different promises for overcomers that Jesus gives to the seven churches.

Rewards of the faithful in the seven churches in *Revelation 2-3* are:
- Eternal life
- Eternal life
- New name/identity
- Messianic rule
- Eternal life
- Eternal presence of God
- Rule and the presence of God.

For the Ephesians, the promise for the overcomers was to eat from the Tree of Life, which would grant eternal life. For the Christians in Smyrna, the promise was that they would not be hurt by the second death, implying that although some of them would be martyred, they would avoid eternal damnation.

For the overcomers in Pergamum, God promised hidden manna, and "a white stone, and on the white stone is written a new name that no one knows except the one who receives it." The meaning of hidden manna is clear. God will give the Christians hidden strength to get through the spiritual wilderness they are in. He is not asking them to leave Pergamum but to endure a lengthy time of difficulties.

But there have been many questions about the meaning of the white stone.

Isaiah 56:3-5 prophesies:

> Do not let the foreigner joined to the Lord say, "The Lord will surely separate me from his people"; and do not let the eunuch say, "I am just a dry tree." For thus says the Lord: "To the eunuchs who keep my sabbaths, who choose the things that please me and hold fast my covenant, I will give, in my house and within my walls, a monument and a name better than sons and daughters; I will give them an everlasting name that shall not be cut off."

In the context of the list that speaks about everlasting rewards, it seems clear that the name the overcomers will receive is everlasting, as prophesied by Isaiah. But what is the meaning of the white stone?

UNDERSTANDING REVELATION

If we follow the hermeneutical principle of seeking the explanation first in the Bible, we must go to Acts, as apart from Revelation, the Greek word for stone or pebble is only mentioned in Acts, and only once.

In *Acts 26:9-11*, when giving a speech in his defence in front of King Agrippa, Paul uses the Greek word *pséphos* (stone, pebble), in the casting of a vote against Christians:

> Indeed, I myself was convinced that I ought to do many things against the name of Jesus of Nazareth. And that is what I did in Jerusalem; with authority received from the chief priests, I not only locked up many of the saints in prison, but I also cast my vote against them when they were being condemned to death. By punishing them often in all the synagogues I tried to force them to blaspheme; and since I was so furiously enraged at them, I pursued them even to foreign cities.

Casting a white stone meant "Yes", but casting a black stone meant "No". Paul, who was being judged by King Agrippa, says that he himself also once judged the followers of Jesus by casting a black stone against them.

Following the theme of overcoming to gain an eternal life, John seems to say that the judgment of God is to give the overcomers an everlasting life with an eternal name, and the giving of the white stone means that they are declared not guilty.

There are alternative explanations to the meaning of the white stone, but they all seem to point to the theme of God giving us an eternal glory through giving us an eternal name. And in the Old Testament, God often renames His people. Their new name will reveal their eternal identity. No matter what people have called us, this is what God will know us as—through eternity. This might be one of the reasons why there will be no jealousy over rewards in heaven; if part of our reward is visible only to God and ourselves privately, it will form part of our eternal identity, but it will be a secret between God and us.

I love the idea that I will have a secret in heaven that will only be known to God and me! Our new name will be the eternal bond that will make my relationship and your relationship with God utterly unique.

REVELATION 2

In *verse 27*, for the overcomers in Thyatira, Jesus will "give authority over the nations" with a clear reference to *Psalm 2:9*. What is interesting is that, just before that, *Psalm 2:8* says:

> Ask of me, and I will make the nations your heritage, and the ends of the earth your possession.

The rule of God's power over the nations is preceded by the promise that the nations will become the inheritance of the Messiah—Jesus. It appears that God does not only promise eternal life but also that the believers will make the nations God's inheritance through the authority of Christ—and then they will rule over nations with authority after they have kept His words until the end. I can find only two places where this authority could be applied: either as spiritual authority to make the nations God's possession or rule in the possible Millennial Kingdom in the end of time.

Verse 27 refers also to *Isaiah 30:14*, which again prophesies about the destruction of Jerusalem because of disobedience, but the following verses promise that one day Zion shall return—and will be blessed with the light of a "sevenfold" sun. But *verse 27* also refers to *Jeremiah 19:11*, which also predicted the earlier destruction of Jerusalem.

John promises to give the overcomers in Thyatira "the morning star", and later on, in *Revelation 22:16*, Jesus is presented as the "bright morning star". *Job 38:7* refers to the morning stars in conjunction with the "heavenly beings". This might be a poetic reference, but it does reflect the common ancient belief that stars were gods.

Isaiah *14:12-15* says:

> How you are fallen from heaven, O Day Star, son of Dawn! How you are cut down to the ground, you who laid the nations low! You said in your heart, "I will ascend to heaven; I will raise my throne above the stars of God; I will sit on the mount of assembly on the heights of Zaphon; I will ascend to the tops of the clouds, I will make myself like the Most High." But you are brought down to Sheol, to the depths of the Pit.

The Hebrew word לילך, translated here as "Day Star", is used only once in the Bible, and it is often translated as Lucifer. Isaiah writes this in the context of Babylon's fall. Lucifer is the Latin name for the planet Venus—the morning star—in the ancient Roman era, and this is the reason why הֵילֵל is also translated as Lucifer. It is called the day star, or more often, the morning star, or the evening star, mainly as although it is a planet, it can sometimes be seen during the daylight.

Why would John use the metaphor of the bright morning star about Jesus? It seems that he uses it in a similar way than Peter.

2 Peter 1:19-21 says:

> So we have the prophetic message more fully confirmed. You will do well to be attentive to this as to a lamp shining in a dark place, until the day dawns and the morning star rises in your hearts. First of all you must understand this, that no prophecy of scripture is a matter of one's own interpretation, because no prophecy ever came by human will, but men and women moved by the Holy Spirit spoke from God.

So, the point Peter makes is that the morning star will rise in the hearts of believers. The meaning is clear: no matter what seems to be happening now, no matter how dark the night, one day, morning will come.

As we have learnt after looking at the Old Testament and Revelation symbolism, it is evident that stars are angels. But why would the early Christians use this kind of language? Why confuse Jesus with angels? Probably because they wanted to claim that Jesus is the right light-bearer, and to connect the morning star with Yahweh, as *Deuteronomy 33:1-3* says:

> This is the blessing with which Moses, the man of God, blessed the Israelites before his death. He said: "The Lord came from Sinai, and dawned from Seir upon us; he shone forth from Mount Paran. With him were myriads of holy ones; at his right, a host of his own. Indeed, O favorite among peoples, all his holy ones were in your charge; they marched at your heels, accepted direction from you."

There are multiple layered meanings here. This begins the Song of Moses that the saints will sing in *Revelation 15:1-4*. So, the Song

REVELATION 2

of Moses is also the Song of the Lamb, as *Revelation 15* also makes clear. The level of linguistic, symbolic, and referential precision is immense in Revelation. Revelation makes the claim that Jesus is the true Morning/Day Star, unlike the goddess Venus. Also, Revelation makes the claim that Jesus is Yahweh who will one day come with myriad of holy ones. Later, *Revelation 19:11-16* will prophesy explicitly about the Second Coming of Jesus in the clouds; here he is already foreshadowing it. By referring to Jesus as the Day Star this way, Revelation makes a claim that the Second Coming of Jesus has always been the plan of God—even when the Law had just been given by Moses. The Law would never be adequate to save, and God knew that even before the Law was given. Also, this way Revelation builds the case for the Law as one of the two witnesses about Jesus.

That alone is mind-blowing. Revelation communicates so much with only a few words! But there is yet another level in the text. In the Roman mythology, Venus was the ancestor of the Roman people, and Julius Caesar, the Roman dictator whose actions led to the demise of the republic and the rise of the Roman Empire, claimed Venus as his ancestor.

Julius Caesar's temple was dedicated to Venus *Genetrix*, and Venus was best known as *Genetrix* ("Begetting Mother") until the death of Emperor Nero in AD 68. Despite the extinction of the Julio-Claudian line with the death of Nero, Venus remained popular with the emperors. For example, Emperor Hadrian completed a temple of Venus in Rome in AD 135.

A comparison of Emperor Domitian with the morning star appears in a poem celebrating his entrance of his consulship in January, AD 95. (Hemer 2001, 5)

The emperor worship was intertwined with the worship of the Begetting Mother, and this was one of the reasons why the veneration of Mary would have been culturally much more acceptable to many Romans than the worship of the crucified Christ.

So, we can see how the early Jewish Christians were reclaiming the concept of the daybreak from the Roman Empire—rather than the emperor bringing the daybreak with the power of Venus, the true daybreak would be brought by Jesus.

UNDERSTANDING REVELATION

This was a collision between two competing claims for divinity, between two radically different sons of god. Revelation is already setting up the central battle between the saints and the Roman Empire that will be described and prophesied in the following chapters.

Christ promises the overcomers in Sardis that they shall be clothed in white garments, and that He will not blot out their name from the Book of Life but will confess their name before His Father and before the angels.

If you are familiar with the Old Testament prophets, it is easy to see the reference to *Isaiah 1:18*:

> "Come now, let us argue it out", says the Lord: "though your sins are like scarlet, they shall be like snow; though they are red like crimson, they shall become like wool."

The concept of the Book of Life appears to have been well known by the early Christians, as Paul also makes a reference in *Philippians 4:3* to people whose names are in the Book of Life.

We can see the similarity between Paul and John's theological outlooks. But the Book of Life appears already in *Psalm 69:28*:

> Let them be blotted out of the book of the living; let them not be enrolled among the righteous.

The idea that both the righteous and the unrighteous are both marked features prominently in Revelation. This idea of marking bodies originates from *Ezekiel 9:3-7*:

> Now the glory of the God of Israel had gone up from the cherub on which it rested to the threshold of the house. The Lord called to the man clothed in linen, who had the writing case at his side; and said to him, "Go through the city, through Jerusalem, and put a mark on the foreheads of those who sigh and groan over all the abominations that are committed in it." To the others he said in my hearing, "Pass through the city after him, and kill; your eye shall not spare, and you shall show no pity. Cut down old men, young men and young women, little children and women, but touch no one who has the mark. And begin at my sanctuary." So they began with the elders who were

REVELATION 2

in front of the house. hen he said to them, "Defile the house, and fill the courts with the slain. Go!" So they went out and killed in the city.

This marking in Ezekiel is an invisible marking to spare from destruction. So, following this principle established by Ezekiel, the mark of the beast must also be an invisible, spiritual marking. It simply means that some people will be marked invisibly for eternal destruction.

For the Philadelphian Christians, God promises that the overcomers will be like pillars in the temple of God, and they will have God's name, the name of New Jerusalem and the new name of Christ written on them.

This continues the theme of Ezekiel and the marking of the saints —not only have they been marked in the Book of Life, but they belong to God eternally, belonging to Him as closely as possible for a created being. They are eternal victors. And unlike with Ezekiel's Jerusalem, it is God Himself and not an angel who will be marking them. There will be no mediator between them and God.

For the overcomers in Laodicea, Jesus promises that they will sit with Him on His throne. They will rule through eternity.

Jesus says in *Matthew 19:28*:

> Truly I tell you, at the renewal of all things, when the Son of Man is seated on the throne of his glory, you who have followed me will also sit on twelve thrones, judging the twelve tribes of Israel.

So, Jesus reminds His followers of the promise He has already given to His first disciples and extends it unequivocally to all overcomers.

With each of the seven churches, the phrase that the Spirit is speaking "to the churches" is repeated. Thich means that the promises made to overcomers in one church are also promises made to all overcomers. They will live forever in the presence of God and rule with Jesus through all eternity. This also means that in every church there will be overcomers.

It is good to remember that before making any sweeping, condemning statements of any groups of Christians, just because we disagree with minor parts of their teaching. There are central issues, such as our confession that Jesus is the Lord, an early Christian confession. There are peripheral doctrines, and if someone disagrees with us about them, it does not automatically make them less of an overcomer. And just because there are grave issues in some churches, it does not mean that every member of those churches has fallen away from Christ. The meek of the land in any church have always served the Lord without bothering themselves about theoretical dilemmas the theologians might fight over; their reward might also be greater than the reward of those debaters.

Smyrna

For Smyrna, Jesus presents Himself as "the first and the last, who was dead, and came to life," foreshadowing the prophecy about persecution that would come from the people who say they are Jews but in fact are the "synagogue" of Satan. The Christians of Smyrna would have affliction for "ten days".

Those who seek historical explanation for Revelation look for a moment of persecution in time of writing. But it seems evident that, regarding Smyrna, Revelation predicts the future rather than accounts for a present situation.

Why does Revelation refer to the synagogue of Satan? Many today find this reference uncomfortable and antisemitic. But John himself was a Jew, so it would be a mistake to read this as an antisemitic statement.

The power balance between the Jews and the Christians was very different then than in the past century or in the Middle Ages. Whereas the Church has witnessed over a thousand years of antisemitism, at this time the Christians themselves belonged to the most vulnerable minority.

I do not think it is wrong to call things by their proper names. If Christians were persecuted by some Jews at this time, Revelation has the right to call it persecution, and in this instance, it claims that these Jews persecuting Christians are not proper Jews, meaning that they were not genuinely following Torah and the Jewish teachings.

In a similar way, it is perfectly permissible to say that Christians are persecuted in many Muslim countries but also that many Muslims are victims of Islamophobia in Western societies. These statements are not contradictory. It is entirely possible for two groups to oppress each other in different circumstances.

In historical research, historical explanations are not generalising but unique, illuminating the specific historical context. And Revelation shows that there was a diversity of relations between different communities when it comes to different cities in Asia Minor. Sometimes the relations were good; at other times they were poor. Good relations produced different problems than the bad ones.

In relation to the Jews, Revelation is a complex book. In one vision, Revelation presents the destruction of Jerusalem as God's judgment, in another vision, the Jewish nation as protected by God in the wilderness, and in yet another vision, it prophesies the return of the Jews to the Promised Land in the end-times.

This complexity of relations between Christians and Jews would be played out in Smyrna in the second century. It was Smyrna in 195 BC that began the deification of the city of Rome with the citizens of Smyrna creating a cult to the goddess Roma when they needed help from Rome. This cult then spread through the whole Roman Empire.

The cult of Rome and its emperors was based on emphasising Rome's invincible strength evident in its military conquests. Asia Minor even adopted a calendar that began each year with the birthday of Augustus: September 23. This decision was made around 9 BC. (Koester 2009, 10, 11)

But clearly, the reference to the synagogue of Satan has nothing to do with the goddess Roma, as some commentators have suggested.

As a large city Smyrna would have attracted both Jews and Christians. The Jews leaving Judea settled in larger cities, rather than the countryside, as did the Christians. (Horsley and Luxford 2016, 150) And by the time of Revelation's writing, the relationship between the Jews and Christians within the Roman Empire had deteriorated.

After the destruction of the Temple in Jerusalem in AD 70, the paying of the Jewish temple tax was transferred from Jerusalem to Jupiter Capitolinus, the most important temple in Rome. This compromise implied recognition of the Roman national deity by the Jews, which allowed the Romans to leave the Jews in peace, as they complied with the Roman religion by paying the tax but allowed the Jews to worship Yahweh only. It was a religious compromise that the Romans were very good at making; you were allowed your own gods if you worshipped the Roman gods. This meant that you had submitted to the empire.

The Jewish Christians, unlike the Gentile Christians, were initially protected from having to worship the Roman gods under the exception rules made for the Jews. As they were considered Jews, they were perceived to honour Jupiter, the chief deity of the Roman state, through paying a tax to him.

The pressure from the emperor cult explains why Christians sought acceptance in the synagogue, and accounts for the proselytization to Judaism in the church of Philadelphia that will be referred to later in Revelation. (Hemer 2001, 8-9)

But after the destruction of the Second Temple, some Jews began to abhor the presence of the Jewish Christians in many synagogues in Asia Minor. Around AD 90, the curse of the Minim was introduced into the "Eighteen Benedictions", the central Jewish prayer given three times a day. This provided a means of detecting Christians in the synagogues. Marcus (2009, 524) provides us with a translation of the curse of the Minim:

> For those doomed to destruction may there be no hope. And may the dominion of arrogance be quickly uprooted in our days. And may the Nazarenes and the heretics be destroyed in a moment and may they be blotted out of the book of life. And may they not be inscribed with the righteous. Blessed are you, O Lord, who subdues the arrogant.

No Nazarene, a follower of Jesus of Nazareth, could recite this prayer, as they would be cursing themselves.

From the rabbinical perspective, the Nazarenes believed in "two powers"—the Father and the Son (ibid., 536), which to the Jews was an apostasy.

The Jewish Christians were also blamed for the destruction of the Second Temple, as they did not participate in the defence of Jerusalem in the uprising but followed the prophetic advice of Jesus for those in Judea to flee to the hills immediately without even collecting their

REVELATION 2

belongings, as instructed in *Matthew 24:16*. This prophecy helped many Christians avoid the siege and the destruction of Jerusalem and the surrounding countryside, and the factitious fighting between the Jews.

The fact remained that the leader of the Jewish Christians, Jesus, had once judged the Second Temple and asked none of His followers to defend it, so many Jews now perceived the Jewish Christians as traitors.

So, Christians had looked for shelter in synagogues because of their exemption from the emperor worship, but some synagogues began forcing Christians out. This made Christians vulnerable to persecution. But this did not take place consistently everywhere, so we have synagogue cities in Revelation which do not even mention persecution by the Jews, as the relationships between Christians and Jews remained good.

At this time, the Jewish Christians still perceived themselves as part of the Jewish synagogue community and true Israel.

What about the prophecy regarding Smyrna having affliction for ten days? We do not have any historical records of persecution in Smyrna immediately after the distribution of the Book of Revelation. But the time periods mentioned in Revelation mostly do not match with chronological time. The theme of affliction reappears with ten crowns of the beast in *Revelation 13*. These ten days of persecution might be linked to the ten crowns, foreshadowing them, especially as numbers function as one of the connecting links between different parts in Revelation.

We begin to understand that these seven churches might not refer only to the actual churches in Asia Minor, but they have another dimension that extends through time. So, it is possible that these ten days are the pre-shadowing of the ten historical seasons of persecution in the Roman Empire that Revelation will later predict. So, Smyrna might also stand prophetically for the whole Church under the Roman persecution.

The *Martyrdom of Polycarp* is a letter accounting the martyrdom of Polycarp, Bishop of Smyrna, who was a disciple of the apostle John. It is the earliest account of Christian martyrdom outside the New Testament.

UNDERSTANDING REVELATION

In AD 155, Polycarp was executed as a criminal in the stadium at Smyrna during the Roman gladiator games. Alexander the Great introduced the Greek games to Hellenise western Asia Minor; the Romans used the blood games to Romanize the same region. The grandest amphitheatre of the empire was the Colosseum in Rome, built for at least 50,000. Elsewhere in the Western Roman Empire, as many as 252 others have been discovered. There was an amphitheatre in Pergamum and Cyzicus, but apparently nowhere else in Asia Minor.

Polycarp and other Christians appeared in the stadium during the interval between the major events. The crime of Christians was that they were "atheists"—they refused to pray to the Roman gods. (Thompson 2002, 27, 30-35)

The Martyrdom of Polycarp accounts:

> While he spoke these and many other like things, he was filled with confidence and joy, and his countenance was full of grace, so that not merely did it not fall as if troubled by the things said to him, but, on the contrary, the proconsul was astonished, and sent his herald to proclaim in the midst of the stadium thrice, "Polycarp has confessed that he is a Christian." This proclamation having been made by the herald, the whole multitude both of the heathen and Jews, who dwelt at Smyrna, cried out with uncontrollable fury, and in a loud voice, "This is the teacher of Asia, the father of the Christians, and the overthrower of our gods, he who has been teaching many not to sacrifice, or to worship the gods." Speaking thus, they cried out, and besought Philip the Asiarch to let loose a lion upon Polycarp. But Philip answered that it was not lawful for him to do so, seeing the shows of wild beasts were already finished. Then it seemed good to them to cry out with one consent, that Polycarp should be burnt alive.

It is debatable whether the letter should be accepted as a true historical account in every detail, but it must reflect some real tensions between the Christians and the Jews in Smyrna.

Tertullian writes around fifty years later in *Ad Martyras* (Part 3, Chapter 1) about martyrs:

REVELATION 2

> Not that I am specially entitled to exhort you; yet not only the trainers and overseers, but even the unskilled, nay, all who choose, without the slightest need for it, are wont to animate from afar by their cries the most accomplished gladiators, and from the mere throng of onlookers useful suggestions have sometimes come; first, then, O blessed, grieve not the Holy Spirit, who has entered the prison with you; for if He had not gone with you there, you would not have been there this day. Do you give all endeavour, therefore, to retain Him; so let Him lead you thence to your Lord. The prison, indeed, is the devil's house as well, wherein he keeps his family.

Tertullian's martyr was modelled as a Christian gladiator, and his account shows how the arena became the central place of martyrdom. Tertullian presents both the arena and the prison that prepares for it as "the devil's house", which has some significance in relation to Pergamum where Satan's throne was, according to *Revelation 2:13*.

What often escapes the modern mind is that the blood games were a thoroughly religious affair. They were a temple of death.

Tertullian writes in *The Apology of Tertullian*, Chapter 15:

> But may be I am to think you more religious in the amphitheatre, where the gods are brought in dancing upon human blood, and upon the dead bodies of criminals; the gods, I say, which supply the fable, unless it be when the poor actors are forced to suffer to the life, and be the very gods themselves. For we have seen an actor truly suffer castration in personating the god Atys of Pessinus; and another playing Hercules in real flames; and among the ludicrous barbarities which are exhibited at noonday, for the entertainment of those who are more greedy of them than dinner. I could not forbear smiling to see Mercury going about with a rod of iron red hot, probing the bodies to fetch out the souls, and Jove's brother Pluto, in like manner, with his mallet in his hand to finish those that were not quite dead, and make them ready for the ferry-boat.

In the arena, the guards dressed like the evil spirits of the dead. Mercury or Pluto watched over the dying and removed the corpses from the arena. (Thompson 2002, 47) The cult of Nemesis in the Roman period was associated with the blood games and the imperial cult. (Tataki 2009, 641)

So, perhaps the double-edged sword of Jesus in reference to Pergamus is there to remind Christians that they were between two swords: one can kill only temporarily, but the other will bring an eternal separation from God.

A century after Polycarp's martyrdom, the empire-wide persecutions of Decius around AD 250 resulted in the apostasy of Euktemon, the bishop of Smyrna. But the elder Pionios went bravely to his death addressing his final words to those "men who boast about Smyrna's beauty ... and those Jews who are present." A graphic description of his crucifixion has been preserved for us in the *Acta Pionii*. (Yamauchi 2003, 62)

We can see the ongoing friction between the Christians and the Jews in this account. The relationship between Christians and the Jews was clearly not good in Smyrna.

When the Ottoman troops massacred thousands of Armenian Christians in Smyrna in September 1922, they initially left the Greek Christians alone, before proceeding to murder the Greeks as well (Morris & Ze'evi 2019, 4-5). But for decades before, when murdering the Armenians, the Ottomans had mostly left the Greeks alone, if they did not shelter any Armenians. Often, the instinct of minorities is to look away to stay out of trouble. But, it seems that in Smyrna in the second century, the Jews did not just look away, but they participated in instilling the trouble.

What makes Polycarp's death remarkable is that, according to church tradition, it was the apostle John who had ordained him to be the bishop of Smyrna.

As John was a true prophet, he would have received prophetic knowledge about people he was in relationship with, especially those he anointed for leadership. That is an integral part of the prophetic ministry. If Christianity is like a tree whose seed has been planted by Jesus, then John must have been praying passionately for some of the branches. This is how spiritual gifts tend to operate. They do not operate in some abstract vacuum but along the lines of compassion.

REVELATION 2

John was prophesying specifically to some of the churches he had been in contact with. Perhaps this revelation was an outcome of his long intercessory ministry over these churches and came as he was praying for them extensively whilst in exile in Patmos.

There are seven letters that have been accepted to have been written by the church father Ignatius, and they can be dated to around AD 115. Three of these letters address some of these seven churches: one was sent to Ephesus, the second to Philadelphia, and the third to Polycarp, who had been ordained by John. In different ways God was preparing Polycarp and the Christians in Smyrna for difficult times and for martyrdom.

Pergamum

When we come to Pergamum, we encounter the One who has "the sharp two-edged sword" acknowledging that the Christians there live where "Satan's throne is", and where Satan "lives". Between these two remarks about Satan's residence is a reminder that Antipas was martyred there.

Some in Pergamum held to the doctrine of Balaam who snared the Israelites to eating things sacrificed to idols and to committing sexual immorality in *Numbers 22-24*. And there were some who held to the doctrine of the Nicolaitans.

Jesus approached Pergamum with a two-edged sword, which is the Word of God; this reveals that the major issues with the church in Pergamum were linked to false doctrines.

The reference to where Satan's throne is and where he lives has been interpreted primarily in four ways. It has been suggested that it refers to:

- the Altar of Zeus and Athena in Pergamum
- the Asklepieion at the outskirts
- Pergamum as a centre of Roman rule in the province of Asia
- the imperial cult temple for Rome and Augustus somewhere in the city. (Friesen 2005, 357)

But all these four suggestions are somewhat unconvincing.

The Altar of Zeus and Athena was built as thanks for a victory over the Gauls in 190 BC. The reason why it has been a popular guess is that in the late nineteenth century the altar was one of the only monuments from Pergamum known to scholars, and the friezes were hauled off and displayed in the Pergamum Museum in Berlin. (ibid., 357, 359) For some conspiracy theorists, the fact that this altar is now located in a city associated with the Nazi Germany has proved tempting, and recently, it was referred to by some Christian Leave campaigners before the Brexit referendum in the UK.

But there is no obvious reason why this specific temple would have been singled out in Revelation.

The second candidate for the throne of Satan is the Pergamene Asklepieion—the healing complex related to the cult of Asklepios. (ibid., 359-360) Again, there is no obvious reason why this healing complex would have been referred to as Satan's throne in Revelation.

Pergamum was not the Roman capital of Asia Minor, as Ephesus was the governmental centre, (ibid., 361) so the theory that this was the reason why it is referred to as Satan's throne has no historical support.

The cult of Roma and Augustus was set up in Pergamum in 29 BC. (Friedrich 2002, 191) But the theory that Pergamum was called Satan's throne because of it being a centre for emperor worship faces some difficulties.

In the time of the writing of Revelation, there were at least thirty-five cities in Asia Minor with temples dedicated to imperial divinities, (ibid., 192) so that would not have been a differentiating factor.

Pergamum's cult was not Asia's only cult for the emperor, and by the time of Emperor Domitian, there were three cults for the emperor in Asia Minor; there probably was not one central imperial temple in Asia Minor. Friesen suggests that it is the hostility leading to the martyrdom of Antipas that Satan's throne is referring to. (Friesen 2005, 363, 365) This seems to be supported by the sandwich structure of the text with the martyrdom placed between two references to Satan.

What is clear is that in John's mind Pergamum had some sort of concentration of demonic power, and this power was able to release serious persecution of Christians.

According to church tradition, Antipas, who had been discipled by John, was roasted to death in a brazen or copper bull in the temple of

REVELATION 2

Artemis. There are many legends around this story, but the kernel of the story is probably true.

We can safely assume that John would have been interceding for people he had been discipling, and this might have been the reason he received the revelation about Pergamum.

So, is the throne of Satan the throne of Artemis? Are we back with the same issue of idolatry that we were dealing with in Ephesus but now with persecution?

I would suggest that these options exclude the only building in Pergamum that fits the bill simply because most scholars do not perceive the religious nature of the blood games in the amphitheatre. But as today with the cutting off the throat of Christians by Islamic extremists, the slaughter of Christians was not just for bloody entertainment but a profoundly religious act.

There was only another amphitheatre in Asia Minor, apart from the one in Pergamum. It was in Cyzicus. But we know nothing about Christianity in the first century Cyzicus. So, if the amphitheatre was Satan's house, there were not that many Christians living near the second Satan's house in Asia Minor—in Cyzicus. And if there were, John probably did not have personal connections to the Christians living there.

As we saw earlier, Tertullian very much saw the amphitheatre and the prison that prepared for it as the devil's house. It was the blood games that made the Roman Empire more horrendous than any earlier empire. And because of the thoroughly religious aspect of these gladiator games, they amounted to a horrendous human sacrifice. It was in the amphitheatre rather than in temples that the Romans sacrificed humans to their gods. And it was in the amphitheatres where many Christians would die in the next centuries.

Tessarae gladiatoris were four-sided prisms of ivory or bone that were bestowed as an honour on gladiators. On the four faces of this white token were inscribed the name referring to the gladiator, a name referring to the patron, a Roman date, and the year in the form of consul's names. (Banducci 2015, 203)

If the house of Satan, using Tertullian's expression, was the amphitheatre, then it would be fitting that the victorious Christian gladiator would receive a white stone, but with a new name. So, the white stone could symbolise either the triumph of the Christian martyr at his death, or as we have seen earlier, that he was declared not guilty. Perhaps it symbolised both.

But the white stone is given to the overcomers in the end of their life, which means that it will reveal the fullness of their identity in God for all eternity. God calls us, but who we are will be made fully manifest only when we enter eternity. That is why it is unwise to define yourself fully by your current roles or gifts. God might be doing something new in your life in the last day of your life! That was the fate of the martyrs.

Thyatira

To the Christians in Thyatira, Jesus comes with the eyes like a flame of fire and with His feet like fine brass. He has many good things to say about the Christians there, but Thyatira is best known for Jesus rebuking them for their acceptance of the woman Jezebel, a false prophetess, who was encouraging them to commit sexual immorality and eat food sacrificed to idols.

Jesus comes to them as the Son of God. This would have been a familiar expression to anyone from Thyatira. The Greek god Apollo, who was the guardian divinity of Thyatira, and the emperor were equally identified as sons of Zeus. And for example, a letter from Emperor Augustus to Ephesus began with "Emperor Caesar, son of the God Julius". (Friedrich 2002, 192)

Apollo was believed to be the son of Zeus and Leto, and Artemis was her twin sister. He was the patron of Delphi and considered to be the prophetic deity that gave revelation to the Delphic oracles, who were all women. Because of that, a female prophetess inspired by a son of god would have been familiar to all people of Thyatira as a prophetess inspired by Apollo. And it seems likely that when Paul referred to the prophetesses in *1 Corinthians 11*, he was rebuking them for bringing pagan prophetic practices to the church.

The appearance of Jesus resembles the man who appeared to Daniel in *Daniel 10:4-6*. This section in Daniel starts a long prophecy, which accounts for events that would take place in the following centuries

REVELATION 2

in the Middle East but also in the end-times. As the Book of Daniel accounts the story of Daniel and his friends remaining obedient to God in Babylon, this message to Thyatira is a reminder that it is possible to live undefiled lives in a pagan culture. It seems evident that this prophetess's prototype was the Queen Jezebel, who enticed Ahab and Israel to follow Baals. Ahab had married Jezebel to have an alliance with the wealthy city of Tyre.

Jezebel's role is often misunderstood, and her seduction is often seen as sexual, but in essence, it was about assimilating to pagan culture, including pagan sexual behaviour, because of trading opportunities and acquiring wealth.

It is difficult to state conclusively what casting her into sickbed and killing her children might mean in Revelation, but it would have been linked to either physical or spiritual death.

Accompanied with her doctrine was the idea of knowing the depths of Satan and through that knowing God better. It seems that Jezebel's doctrine was linked to an early version of "hyper-grace". Paul refers to that kind of justifying of sin in *Romans 6:1*:

> What then are we to say? Should we continue in sin in order that grace may abound?

This was a complete misinterpretation of Jesus's words to a woman who washed His feet with her tears in *Luke 7:47*:

> Therefore, I tell you, her sins, which were many, have been forgiven; hence she has shown great love. But the one to whom little is forgiven, loves little.

By sinning more and more extensively the followers of Jezebel would love Jesus more, they reasoned. They would know God's grace more abundantly, as grace would abound in the process of sinning.

Associated with Thyatira was the unusual prominence of trade guilds. As we have learnt before, the Jews were the only people group that had been granted exemption for trading in the Roman Empire without having to worship the Roman gods. Initially, Christians were perceived as a Jewish sect and included in this exemption, although converts from paganism would have faced difficulties.

UNDERSTANDING REVELATION

By the time of writing of Revelation, many of the Jewish Christians had already been expelled from the synagogues, and Christians were now a distinct group with no legal exemption from the religion of the empire. It seems evident that the historical figure Revelation refers to as Jezebel had come up with a doctrine that justified taking part in trading within the pagan temple areas. Her theology, as spread by her counterparts in the Thyatira church, would have been especially attractive to Christians who were in the workers' guilds. To reject guild membership would cause one to suffer economic deprivation. However, to be part of a trade guild required participation in its pagan religious festivities.

The temptation to compromise one's Christian beliefs must have been immense for many church members. So, many Christians in Thyatira were willing to compromise with their sexuality and worship because of money, and Jezebel enticed them to do that.

The teaching of Balaam in Pergamum and the teaching of Jezebel produced similar outcomes: idolatry and fornication. Idolatry was the price of fully partaking in the Greco-Roman economic system.

In Galatia, many Gentile Christians had become attracted to Judaism, and the same had happened in Philippi. Paul wrote in *Philippians 3:2*:

> Beware of the dogs, beware of the evil workers, beware of those who mutilate the flesh!

The main attraction of Judaism was not the Law but the economic protection that circumcision would bring. The early Christians could compromise in two opposite ways—by becoming Jews or by worshipping idols. In both cases, this compromise would bring an economic advantage. When pagans converted to Christianity, they would have found themselves at least partially cut away from the economic system of the empire. Through circumcision they would have been accepted into the Jewish community as converts and protected by special rights given to the Jews in the Roman Empire. But in Thyatira they chose to accept a doctrine that enabled them to worship as Christians but also to attend the feasts of the pagan

REVELATION 2

temple cults. This was the temptation of Jezebel in the ancient Israel: to worship Baals alongside Yahweh—mainly because of the economic benefits it could bring, as the surrounding nations also worshipped Baals.

It is likely that knowing the deep things of Satan involved participating in the pagan temple cults. As we have learnt, Jesus's warning to Thyatira begins with terms that were also used to describe Apollo, which strengthens the case that Jezebel was a proponent of some level of syncretism.

The temples for Apollo were oracular shrines. Apollo was represented by Pythia, the Oracle of Delphi, who was his priestess. She established contact with Apollo through his sacred tree, the laurel, by holding a laurel branch. (Huffmon 2007, 450, 454) Apollo was considered to possess Pythia. As the possessed and chosen instrument of Apollo, she was seen to be the conduit of divine knowledge. (Maurizio, 1995, 71, 75, 84)

Jezebel's prophesying was not an isolated phenomenon but part of a trend that had already begun before the birth of Christianity. The Jewish-Christian *Sibylline Oracles* combine Judaism and Hellenism. Their writing began by the Jews in Alexandria in the second century BC, but the whole collection was written and modified over the following centuries. They are an example of syncretism through the work of prophetesses.

Sibyls and the sibylline tradition themselves were a wholly Greco-Roman invention. The Greco-Roman prophecy had two sometimes competing and sometimes coordinating streams, the Apollo-inspired oracle at Delphi, and the ecstatic, cryptic sibyls scattered across the Mediterranean world. To assume the mantle of the sibyl was to tap into one of the most significant authorities of the pagan world. *Sibylline Oracles* drew mythology from both the Jewish and Greek cultures, mixing the account of the Titans with stories of Babel and the Flood. Many Greeks referred to the Jews as philosophers by birth, as they believed in one God. Cities minted coins in honour of sibyls. (Gabrielson 2015, 214, 219, 220, 221, 225)

A female prophetess, confessing Christ but also some Jewish beliefs alongside the Greek beliefs would have been entirely acceptable to the Greeks in Asia Minor.

UNDERSTANDING REVELATION

Over the years I have had many conversations with a Hindu friend, and he truly respects my faith in Jesus. But for him Christ is merely one acceptable road amongst others. There is no exclusivity, and if you come from Hindu tradition, you can easily confuse Christ with Krishna, the Hindu god. But the situation changes when Christians preach radical exclusivity of salvation only by Christ.

In *1 Corinthians 1:23* Paul says that he preaches the Christ crucified, which was, according to him, foolishness to the Greeks. It was not Christ who was foolishness to the Greeks but the crucified Christ. And today, we must take heed of this warning, as increasingly, both the left and the right wing of the Church have begun to preach Christ that is acceptable to their constituencies but removes the foolishness of the cross.

So, Jezebel could wield great authority in the church, as she could draw her strength both from the Greek and the Jewish traditions. There were many reasons why the Christians in Thyatira would have found her message attractive. But, ultimately, following her would lead to great distress, as it would severe Christians from the life of Christ.

REVELATION 3

Sardis

Revelation 3 begins with a letter to Sardis, which used to be the capital of the kingdom of Lydia before the Roman takeover. It was the place where metallurgists first discovered how to separate gold from silver, and it is known as the city where modern currency was invented.

In AD 17, during the reign of Tiberius, a massive earthquake caused havoc in twelve prominent cities of Asia, with Sardis hit the hardest.

Sardis had a high-profile Jewish community around the time John wrote the letter. (Horsley & Luxford 2016, 150) The settlement of Jews occurred at least as early as 210 BC when Antiochus III brought two thousand Jewish families from Babylon. The Jews had their own laws, and they decided their own affairs. The third-century synagogue was converted from part of a large civic complex in the heart of the city, and it had capacity of over a thousand people. (Gaston 2006, 17-20) This reflects the prominent position of the Jews in the city.

The Jewish community in Sardis was recognised and its practices approved. By the third century there were at least eight Jewish members in the city council, and there were Gentiles that had converted to Judaism. (Ascough 2006, 246)

We know only a little about the Christian community before Melito, the Bishop of Sardis who died around AD 180. He made a petition to Emperor Marcus Aurelius, presenting Christianity as a philosophy that had contributed to the greatness of the Roman Empire. Melito is the first known to have made an argument about the inter-relatedness of the Church and the Roman history. (Aasgaard 2006, 162, 163) This implies that Christians had positioned themselves as a group like Judaism—as respectable citizens of the empire.

In Sardis, there seems to have been cooperation between the Jews and Christians when it came to festive dates. (Ascough 2006, 247) In Sardis, which was not too far from Smyrna, Christians lived mostly in peaceful coexistence with the Jews and pagans and in conformity with the Roman Empire. Also, unlike in Smyrna, the relationships between the Jews and Christians never really deteriorated. Perhaps because of this lack of struggle, the church in Smyrna grew initially, but its growth was not enduring.

Architecturally, there are only a few Christian remains. The remnants of a Christian basilica (ca. AD 340-350) have been excavated half a kilometre from the city centre, outside the city walls. A small fourth-century chapel has been detected adjacent to an Artemis temple. (Aasgaard 2006, 173) It seems evident that in Sardis and not just in Ephesus Mary was being merged with Artemis.

Christians would have benefited from the favour the Jews had in the city, and by celebrating their holy days when the Jews celebrated theirs, Christians would not have stood out as much as in some other cities in the Roman Empire. So, Sardis became the church that was acceptable to the Roman Empire. It presented discipleship without major struggles or persecution.

Today, there are many Sardis-like churches that submit the call to follow Jesus under the authority of whichever state they serve. And Sardis helped to develop the "theology of the empire", rational reasons for assimilation and conformity.

It seems that Sardis found reasons to rationalise everything. The Christians of Sardis, much like the Jews, were sensible people. They knew how to balance things. They were the Christians acceptable in the wider society. They caused no major offences. That is why we know very little of them. For the call to follow Jesus has never been for the balanced minds; it has always been unconditional and radical.

On surface, the church of Sardis was doing well. But the Christians were only doing well in their minds and in the eyes of the surrounding society because they were asleep and at the point of death. They fitted a society that was spiritually dead rather too well. Today, much of the Western Christendom looks like Sardis. We are acceptable in society, but only because we disregard parts of the gospel that are not palatable to the sensibilities of our seemingly tolerant societies.

Philadelphia

Philadelphia is one of the only two churches out of seven not reprimanded at any level by Jesus. The other one was Smyrna. The difference between Smyrna and Philadelphia is that Smyrna was predicted to suffer from major persecution whilst Philadelphia seemed exempt from it. This shows that it is possible for Christians to please God even when they are not persecuted!

Jesus promises to open a door for the Philadelphian Christians and that some of the Jews would come to know Him through them. It is to the Philadelphians that Jesus promises New Jerusalem, possibly contrasting that promise with the weak status of Christians in the city. Perhaps this was a church consisting mainly of non-citizens of both the city and the Roman Empire. On earth, they were insignificant, but in heaven, they would be important citizens.

Jesus promises that the Philadelphian Christians would be protected from the great trial that would come on the earth.

Initially, there do not seem to be many clues for why Jesus commended the church in Philadelphia for their obedience, apart from the fact that they had persevered. But we can find some clues from the church history.

According to Eusebius, the first church historian, there was a prophetic movement that grew in Philadelphia, which later diverged into Montanism (Hemer 2001, 5). Montanism was known by its followers as the New Prophecy. This movement began late second century and survived until the sixth century.

Montanus, the founder of the movement, was associated with the area around Philadelphia, and he had an interest in Revelation and especially the letter to Philadelphia. (Trevett 1989, 314)

In Eusebius's *Church History*, Book V, Chapter 17, Eusebius contrasts what he considers the false prophecy of the Montanist school with the prophets in Philadelphia. He writes:

UNDERSTANDING REVELATION

> But the *false prophet* falls into an *ecstasy*, in which he is without shame or *fear*. Beginning with purposed *ignorance*, he passes on, as has been stated, to involuntary *madness* of *soul*.

Eusebius contrasts the Montanist prophets with Agabus, Judas, Silas and the daughters of Philip in the Book of Acts, and with Ammia in Philadelphia. We know very little of Ammia, apart from the fact that she was a prophetess linked to Philadelphia and not considered a heretic by the Church that slowly began to establish what would later become the Roman Catholic ecclesiastical structures.

Montanism emphasised the importance and intensity of spiritual gifts. Ecstatic trances were the main reason for dissension between Montanists and Catholics. Montanism included speaking in tongues, and Montanists recorded a huge number of prophecies in their prophetic books. (Wypustek 1997, 277, 278, 280)

The Passion of Saint Perpetua, Saint Felicitas, and Their Companions is one of the oldest and most notable early Christian texts. It contains a first-person prison diary of the young mother and martyr Perpetua. Perpetua and Felicity were Christian martyrs in the early third century. They were put to death along with others at Carthage in the Roman province of Africa.

The text, which many consider to be Montanist, says:

> If the former examples of faith served both as a witness to the grace of God and for the bringing about of the upbuilding of humankind, and they were set forth in letters precisely because of this, so that by reading them, re-presenting as it were the events, God might be honoured and humankind be comforted, why should not also new documents fitting to both these ends be produced? At least for this reason, that they too will sometime be old and necessary for those who come after, though in their own present time they are reckoned to be of less authority because of this presumed respect for antiquity. But let those who judge the one power of the one Holy Spirit on the basis of times and ages consider this: that the more recent things are to be thought the greater, precisely because they are the newest, in accordance with the superiority of grace that has been decreed for the last ages of the world.
>
> "For in the latter days, the Lord says, I shall pour out from

my Spirit on all flesh, and their sons and daughters shall prophesy; and on my slaves and maidservants I shall pour out from my Spirit; and the young shall see visions and the old shall dream dreams."[Acts 2:17–18]

Therefore we too, who both acknowledge and honour the promise of new prophecies and equally the new visions, and reckon the rest of the deeds of power of the Holy Spirit to be for the use of the Church (to which the same Spirit was sent to administer all gifts to all, as the Lord distributes to each), necessarily both write and celebrate them in reading for the glory of God, lest any weakness of faith or despair should deem that the grace of the Godhead dwelt only among those of old, whether in the dignity of martyrdoms, or in that of revelations, since God always works those things which he promised as a witness to unbelievers and as a benefit to believers. (Parvis 2009, 367-368)

The book verbalises a belief in the unceasing revelation and leaves the door open to the teaching that new prophecies could have a similar authority than the books and letters gathered in the New Testament.

Montanism is not dissimilar to many modern-day false prophetic movements, such as Branhamism, which has elevated the sermons of William Branham at the equal level with the Bible and even the arbiter over the Bible.

In the book, Perpetua demands the right for the Christians not to be dressed in the robes of priests of Saturn and priestesses of Ceres while in the arena. (ibid., 371) This again demonstrates the thoroughly religious nature of the killing of Christians in the amphitheatres.

Montanism took many elements from Revelation but eventually distorted them by pushing them too far; many heresies are the outcome of unhealthy focus on a sound idea found in the Bible.

But it seems clear that Philadelphia had at John's time a healthy Christian community that still practised the gifts of the Spirit. And this set it on collision course with the church leaders that sought to give the apostolic authority to bishops.

Ignatius, the bishop of Antioch, wrote *The Epistle to the Philadelphians* around AD 110, not long after the writing of Revelation. The epistle seeks to reinforce the bishop's authority over the congregations. In those days, a bishop would have been an overseer of many house churches, and Paul refers to overseers in many of his letters. The ecclesiastical role of the bishop evolved from the role of the overseer of house churches. Ignatius writes in Chapter 3 of his letter:

> For as many as are of God and of Jesus Christ are also with the bishop. And as many as shall, in the exercise of repentance, return into the unity of the Church, these, too, shall belong to God, that they may live according to Jesus Christ.

In Chapter 7 he asks the Philadelphians to "do nothing without the bishop".

In Ignatius's time some Philadelphian Christians were asking questions about the authority of leaders and the Scriptures which would be paralleled in later decades among the Montanists. (Trevett 1989, 327)

Ignatius supported the idea of monarchical priesthood, which would eventually lead to the creation of papacy in Rome.

Contrasting Philadelphia with the churches that would later develop into fully ecclesiastical hierarchies is helpful, as it helps us to see that in Revelation Jesus saw the healthy use of spiritual gifts and lack of religious hierarchies as something that was praiseworthy. After all, He called us to be brothers and sisters and not a hierarchical institution.

We begin to see the reasons behind the institutionalised, hierarchical church quenching the gifts—if you cannot do anything without the permission of the bishop, it will quench the freedom that is necessary for the operation of spiritual gifts.

Paul writes in *2 Corinthians 3:17*:

> Now the Lord is the Spirit, and where the Spirit of the Lord is, there is freedom.

It seems that there was a level of opposition in Philadelphia against ecclesiastical hierarchy. This raises questions about the relevancy of the message to the seven churches for different church ages. Applying this to the contemporary Church, the Philadelphian churches would be outside any state religious system, and they would practise what is called the priesthood of all believers, seeking to follow the principles of equality as much as it is practically possible. Many a church preaches equality of believers but is in practice led by a group of professional church ministers and operates as a hierarchical institution.

Laodicea

The church of Laodicea is the last in the list of the seven churches. The one thing most Christians know about Laodicea is that the Laodiceans were called lukewarm by Jesus. The most common explanation for the reference to being lukewarm is that there were no freshwater springs at Laodicea, so they had to utilise aqueducts, and water came from hot springs. By the time it reached the city, the water would have been lukewarm, neither beneficently hot nor refreshingly cold.

But this explanation does not seem historically accurate, and Koester is not convinced of it. The hot springs were located at Hierapolis, about six miles north of Laodicea. They had high mineral content. The metaphor of coldness is usually related to Colossae, which was about eleven miles east of Laodicea and enjoyed an ample supply of fresh water. But according to Koester, this explanation cannot be correct, since the ancient descriptions of the hot springs do not suggest that their waters were desired for drinking. For example, Strabo, a Greek geographer, philosopher, and historian thought that water from Laodicea was better for drinking than water from Hierapolis. According to Strabo, it tended to calcify like the water from the hot springs, but it was fresh. There is no evidence that the water from Laodicea was thought to be undrinkable. Especially the water from the Roman aqueduct was perceived as fine water and provided water in addition to the two rivers serving the city. And Hierapolis was in the north, but the aqueduct approached the city from the south, so this water could not have come from Hierapolis but had another source. (Koester 2003, 409-411)

So, rather than focusing on local topography, Koester looks for answers from dining and drinking culture, which fits John's metaphor perfectly.

A chilled beverage was seen positively, as snow was used to chill wine. Also, heated wine became a common feature for dinners in the

UNDERSTANDING REVELATION

Roman times. When it comes to lukewarmth, the *Life of Aesop* 2-3 tells of using lukewarm water to induce vomiting. Also, the evidence does not suggest that wealth characterised Laodicea any more than other cities. The eye salve mentioned, for example, was not a local product but commonly marketed and produced in the Roman Empire. (ibid., 413-414, 416, 422)

The Laodiceans did not seem to struggle with any major issues linkd to idols or false prophets and doctrines. They were not rebuked for idolatry. But according to Jesus, the Laodiceans thought they had already become rich when they were really poor. Perhaps Paul can give us some clues about what this meant.

Paul writes in *Colossians 1:27*:

> To them God chose to make known how great among the Gentiles are the riches of the glory of this mystery, which is Christ in you, the hope of glory.

This letter is significant in relation to Laodiceans, as in *Colossians 2:1* Paul writes:

> For I want you to know how much I am struggling for you, and for those in Laodicea, and for all who have not seen me face to face.

Colossians 4:16 also says:

> And when this letter has been read among you, have it read also in the church of the Laodiceans; and see that you read also the letter from Laodicea.

Unfortunately, Paul's letter to the Laodiceans has not been preserved to us. But the Laodiceans would have been very familiar with Paul's letter to the Colossians, as its *chapter 4* shows that it has been written to those in Colossae, Laodicea, and Hierapolis with the three cities located only a few miles from each other. What Paul's letters show is that many of the churches in the Greek world had similar problems.

Paul writes in *1 Corinthians 4:8-13*:

REVELATION 3

Already you have all you want! Already you have become rich! Quite apart from us you have become kings! Indeed, I wish that you had become kings, so that we might be kings with you! For I think that God has exhibited us apostles as last of all, as though sentenced to death, because we have become a spectacle to the world, to angels and to mortals. We are fools for the sake of Christ, but you are wise in Christ. We are weak, but you are strong. You are held in honor, but we in disrepute. To the present hour we are hungry and thirsty, we are poorly clothed and beaten and homeless, and we grow weary from the work of our own hands. When reviled, we bless; when persecuted, we endure; when slandered, we speak kindly. We have become like the rubbish of the world, the dregs of all things, to this very day.

Unlike Laodicea, located in Asia Minor, Corinth was in the southcentral Greece. We do not have any biblical or historical references for John ever visiting Corinth. But it seems that the churches in Laodicea and Corinth were both taken over with the teaching that they were already living in the fullness of the Kingdom. In contemporary terms, the Laodiceans might have confessed "Christ only" and not been tempted away by the Greco-Roman gods, but theirs seemed to be a prosperity gospel not dissimilar to the Corinthian one, which at least based on Paul's criticism did not acknowledge suffering and want as part of legitimate Christian experience.

Like Corinth, Laodicea was one of the churches that had been influenced by Paul's teaching. Paul teaches in *Ephesians 2:6-7* that God has:

> Raised us up with him and seated us with him in the heavenly places in Christ Jesus, so that in the ages to come he might show the immeasurable riches of his grace in kindness toward us in Christ Jesus.

Paul's teaching about the kingly position of the believers would certainly have reached Laodicea, and it appears that the Laodiceans had decided that they had already received that kingly position in fullness. Hence, I think most readers misunderstand the Laodicean problem. In the eyes of many Christians today, the church of Laodicea might have had looked like a particularly strong church, as they had no major issues with idolatry. But theirs was the gospel of success and prosperity. Theirs was all the Kingdom now and not later.

Church history gives us some further clues. Bishop Sagaris of Laodicea died as martyr in AD 166, and in the end of the third century, several church members also died as martyrs, so there would be some persecution in future. But the real issue was related to the church's proximity with the Jewish community. According to Josephus, the Jewish historian, Laodicea had a large Jewish community. Near Laodicea lies Eumeneia, a city where there is evidence for close ties between the Jewish and Christian communities. In Eumeneia, it is often difficult to even distinguish between Jewish and Christian inscriptions. In the fourth century, a church council took place in Laodicea, and Canon 37 from the council states that the Christian faithful of Laodicea attended Jewish feasts and synagogue worship, and they kept the Jewish Sabbath. The worship of the archangel Michael had also become widespread in area. The cult of angels became popular in Asia Minor because the Most High was considered so far removed from the world of men that intermediaries were called upon. These intermediaries were called *theos*, *theos angelos* or *theos angelikos*. The canons of Laodicea show how far the syncretistic activities of the Christian faithful with the Jews had spread—they included angel worship and magic. (Hosang 2008, 79, 84, 86, 94, 97, 104-106)

In the end of Revelation, John himself makes the mistake of attempting to worship an angel, but the angel rebukes him, asking him to worship God alone. We begin to see the consequences of the Laodicean boasting of their spirituality and their spiritual experiences. In later days, it had led them astray in two directions: to embrace the Jewish legalism and to embrace their spiritual experiences. So, the Laodiceans boasted that they were rich in spiritual experience, but Jesus said that they were poor. But because the spirituality they followed had a Jewish veneer, they perceived it as higher spirituality.

It is important to understand the letters to the seven churches first in their first-century context before applying them today.

Revelation 1-3 focuses on the Church on earth, beginning from the time of writing. It focuses on the current situation in John's time but

REVELATION 3

foreshadows the later developments in the Church prophesied later in the book. Apart from the introduction to Revelation, these chapters all explain one revelatory vision that John saw.

If the Kingdom of God is like the mustard seed, which becomes the largest of trees, then these seven churches must be some of the branches in the tree. Some scholars have found seven different church eras in the seven churches, but following the tree analogy, it is more likely that these seven branches represent all churches through different eras of church history. So, they are relevant to churches in any generation, when read reflectively and with understanding. Perhaps one contemporary church has elements that feature in more than one of these seven churches, as the growth of the branches might not have followed a straight trajectory.

The Second Vision

REVELATION 4

The second vision beginning in *Revelation 4* will give us a different perspective—of what is happening in heaven. It is vital to grasp that in prophetic writing a new section does not always follow the previous section chronologically or linearly. Instead, this begins a new vision. So, the events described in *Revelation 4* do not necessarily happen after the events in *Revelation 3*, but they can precede, coincide with, overlap with, or follow them.

Revelation 4 begins with a door opened in heaven. John hears a voice, which asks him to come up to heaven to find out what will happen after this.

This is clearly a new vision, although it has been written as continuation of the first vision. Perhaps John saw this without disruption from the first vision, but the perspective changes so abruptly that it must nevertheless be approached as a separate vision. "After this" only tells that John saw this after what he had seen in the preceding chapters. There might have been a long, short or no interval at all between seeing these visions.

The door to heaven opens—now we will see what is happening in heaven. Amongst the worshippers are twenty-four elders. These must represent both Israel and the Church, as Revelation concerns the history, the present and the future of both the Church and Israel. John has already written about both Israel and the Church, and Israel has twelve tribes and the Church twelve apostles, with both twelves reappearing in different segments of Revelation.

So, it seems entirely reasonable to assume that twenty-four elders refer to both the twelve tribes of Israel and the twelve apostles, not least because according to *Revelation 21*, New Jerusalem will have twelve foundations with the names of the twelve apostles, and the gates will bear the names of Israel's tribes.

The purpose of God has been manifested by Israel and the Church, and His plans for them are intertwined. First, there was a covenant with Israel and then there was a covenant with the Church. It is this New Covenant which provides the foundation to New Jerusalem. Nevertheless, twenty-four elders demonstrate that God's plan for Israel is an eternal and not just temporal plan. The saved will include some people from Israel, and their roles are somewhat different from the roles of the saved Gentiles, although both share in the same eternal inheritance.

Our God is a covenant-keeping God, and Revelation outlines how God will fulfil every covenantal word He has spoken to humanity.

In *verse 5*, seven lamps are burning in front of the throne, representing the seven spirits of God. This presents the unity of God the Father, the Son, and the Holy Spirit visually.

The Father is seated on the throne, the Son will soon come to Him as the Lamb, and the seven spirits of God we have already encountered in *Revelation 1:4* are also present.

Some scholars claim that the doctrine of the Trinity is a post-biblical theological invention, but here we have a sophisticated visualised theology of the Trinity presented to us. The Father is on the throne, His seven spirits are burning before the throne, and the Son of God has been anointed by these seven spirits—the Holy Spirit. Earlier on in Revelation, the Son of God has already been identified with the Father. They are One and yet three distinctive Persons.

But what is this sea of glass, like crystal, in front of the throne in *verse 6*? Revelation is a book full of symbols. John had to enter heaven symbolically through a door, and the sea of transparent glass symbolises that God can see everything that happens below Him on earth. We cannot see what happens in heaven unless God permits it by opening a door, but He can see all things that are taking place on earth.

This is a reference to *Ezekiel 1:22*:

> Over the heads of the living creatures there was something like a dome, shining like crystal, spread out above their heads.

REVELATION 4

In this instance, the visions of Ezekiel and John are similar; only God visits Ezekiel on earth whereas John visits God in heaven. That is why the architecture in the vision is slightly different with the crystal sea appearing above the creatures when they are on earth rather than below them when they are in heaven.

This revelation of God's omniscience will be reinforced by the four living creatures that are also referred to in *Ezekiel 1*.

The clue for the identity of the four living creatures singing that the Lord Almighty is holy comes in the worship song of the twenty-four elders who lay their crowns before God on the throne in *verse 11*:

> You are worthy, our Lord and God, to receive glory and honor and power, for you created all things, and by your will they existed and were created.

The worship songs in Revelation tend to point towards the reason for worship; the worship song of the elders explains what the four creatures are—they are all the created things.

The creatures have eyes "around and within". This means that God can see everything that is happening in the universe He has created, including our innermost being. Nothing in the universe remains hidden from Him.

He is the all-seeing God.

Revelation 4 begins the section where everything we see happens in heaven. It provides a transition to the events that will shape eternity in *Revelation 5*.

REVELATION 5

Revelation 5 continues the vision of heaven begun in *Revelation 4*. The One sitting on the throne has a scroll that has been sealed with seven seals. This scroll has writing on the inside and on the outside. The writing on the outside means that some of the scroll has already been readable to us. There are still mysteries hidden in the scroll, but some of the revelation has already been revealed to us by the Old Testament prophets who could read the outside. But now time has come to read what has been written on the inside. But what has been written has been written long ago, perhaps even before the creation of the world.

1 Peter 1:10-12 says:

> Concerning this salvation, the prophets who prophesied of the grace that was to be yours made careful search and inquiry, inquiring about the person or time that the Spirit of Christ within them indicated when it testified in advance to the sufferings destined for Christ and the subsequent glory. It was revealed to them that they were serving not themselves but you, in regard to the things that have now been announced to you through those who brought you good news by the Holy Spirit sent from heaven—things into which angels long to look!

The Old Testament prophets were able to investigate this scroll from the outside, but now it has been opened, and we can read the inside, the whole revelation. But even the angels have been longing to see what is written in the inside.

The vision takes us to the moment when the scroll is yet to be opened. An angel is calling for anyone who is worthy to break the seals

UNDERSTANDING REVELATION

and open the scroll. John begins to weep as there is no one worthy to open it. But one of the elders asks him not to weep, for "the Lion of the tribe of Judah, the Root of David" has triumphed.

Hosea 11:10-11 prophesies about God as the Lion of Judah:

> They shall go after the Lord, who roars like a lion; when he roars, his children shall come trembling from the west. They shall come trembling like birds from Egypt, and like doves from the land of Assyria; and I will return them to their homes, says the Lord.

Genesis 49 accounts Jacob's blessing for his sons with focus on Judah in verses *9 and 10*:

> Judah is a lion's whelp; from the prey, my son, you have gone up. He crouches down, he stretches out like a lion, like a lioness—who dares rouse him up? The scepter shall not depart from Judah, nor the ruler's staff from between his feet, until tribute comes to him; and the obedience of the peoples is his.

The blessing appears to contain a messianic prophecy. Again, the Law is a witness about Christ.

The root of David refers to the prophecies of Zechariah. Root here means "stock", "family", "descendant", hence, "the Root of David" is that which descended from David, not that which David descended from. *Zechariah 3:6-10* says:

> Then the angel of the Lord assured Joshua, saying "Thus says the Lord of hosts: If you will walk in my ways and keep my requirements, then you shall rule my house and have charge of my courts, and I will give you the right of access among those who are standing here. Now listen, Joshua, high priest, you and your colleagues who sit before you! For they are an omen of things to come: I am going to bring my servant the Branch. For on the stone that I have set before Joshua, on a single stone with seven facets, I will engrave its inscription, says the Lord of hosts, and I will remove the guilt of this land in a single day. On that day, says the Lord of hosts, you shall invite each other to come under your vine and fig tree."

REVELATION 5

Joshua was the first priest chosen to be the High Priest during the reconstruction of the Jewish Temple after the return of the Jews from exile in Babylon.

Zechariah 6:9-13 says:

> The word of the Lord came to me: "Collect silver and gold from the exiles—from Heldai, Tobijah, and Jedaiah—who have arrived from Babylon; and go the same day to the house of Josiah son of Zephaniah. Take the silver and gold and make a crown, and set it on the head of the high priest Joshua son of Jehozadak; say to him: 'Thus says the Lord of hosts: "Here is a man whose name is Branch: for he shall branch out in his place, and he shall build the temple of the Lord. It is he that shall build the temple of the Lord; he shall bear royal honor, and shall sit upon his throne and rule. There shall be a priest by his throne, with peaceful understanding between the two of them."'"

When it comes to the Branch, Zechariah's prophecy in *3:6-10* is intriguing, as although it is the High Priest Joshua who is being crowned, the prophecy seems to contain another prophecy within about God removing the iniquity of the land in one single day. What is happening to Joshua is significant, but what is even more significant than the directive prophecy regarding Joshua is the prophecy it contains; what God will do for Joshua will begin a development that will end with the fulfilment of the prophecy within.

We can see how economically Revelation has been written—by referring to the Lion of the tribe of Judah and the Root of David, Revelation brings together the theme of the return of the Jews to God, the removal of iniquity, and the building of the temple, and links it to what is taking place in heaven.

Yeshua—Jesus—was a common alternative of the name Joshua, meaning "the Lord is my salvation" during the Second Temple Israel. It also appears in some books of the Jewish Bible. For example, Joshua the High Priest is referred to both as Joshua and *Yeshua* in the Jewish Bible.

This develops the theme of Jesus as the High Priest but gives it a new dimension. Jesus is the one who will restore the temple; only the temple is no more the temple in Jerusalem, which has been destroyed by the Romans, but the presence of God amongst people. This will happen partially through the Church but will be made manifest fully in heaven.

The slaughtered Lamb has seven horns and seven eyes, which are the seven spirits of God that symbolise God's perfection—the Lamb is God. Again, the triune nature of God is made clear. The Lamb is not only anointed by the seven spirits of God, but the seven spirits of God are clearly revealed as integral to His Person.

This gradual unfolding is typical to a narrative; to get the full picture of what Revelation says about nearly anything, you will have to read through the whole book from beginning to end. This technique of narrative foreshadowing rarely summarises anything in one clear sentence.

A medieval theologian influenced by Greek philosophy would conclude with one sentence that God is triune and then seek to defend that argument. But with narrative explaining that Revelation utilises, you will need to read the whole narrative to conclude that God is triune, and understand what it means.

Matthew 13:10-12 says,

> Then the disciples came and asked him, "Why do you speak to them in parables?" He answered, "To you it has been given to know the secret of the kingdom of heaven, but to them it has not been given. For to those who have, more will be given, and they will have an abundance; but from those who have nothing, even what they have will be taken away."

Visions, dreams, and parables are all symbolically loaded forms of communication. They must be interpreted differently than theological argumentation.

The worship song in verses *9 and 10* explains what has happened: Jesus has purchased people for God from every tribe, language and nation and made them to be a kingdom and priests who will reign on the earth.

Then the whole universe including the saints worships the Lamb.

We can see again how Revelation is not meant to be interpreted chronologically as one prophecy about the future. In time of its writing,

REVELATION 5

the Lamb has already broken the seals and opened the scroll: this was the moment of crucifixion and resurrection. It is chronologically in the past, so Revelation is looking backwards. But when it comes to world history, this is the most significant event of all time, and it transforms the meaning of the past and not just the future.

This vision is quite clear in meaning, and it provides a welcome break from the many mysteries of the book.

REVELATION 6

Revelation 6 is continuation of the vision in *Revelation 5*. It begins with the Lamb opening the first of the seven seals. This is the first consequence of His victory on the cross, and rather fittingly, a white horse with a rider who holds a crown and has a bow rides out as a conqueror bent on conquest.

There is a clear internal reference to a white horse in *Revelation 19*, where Jesus wearing many crowns rides on a white horse with the armies of heaven following him.

The first consequence of the Lamb opening the scroll is the limited advancement of the Kingdom. This is caused by the breaking of the first seal. The good news has been released on the earth, and people will be won to the Kingdom from every tribe and nation. But only in the end of time Christ will appear with the armies of heaven to exercise total authority over the people of the earth.

The second consequence of opening the scroll is the release of a rider with a red fiery horse. He is given the power to take peace from the earth. This is caused by the breaking of the second seal.

The third horseman riding on the black horse brings famine on the earth, but he is asked not to "damage the olive oil and the wine." Whilst many people will struggle to find payment for their barley, others will live in luxury. This is caused by the breaking of the third seal.

The breaking of the fourth seal gives the power for the pale horse to bring death "over a fourth of the earth, to kill with sword, famine, and pestilence, and by the wild animals of the earth." This is caused by the breaking of the fourth seal.

UNDERSTANDING REVELATION

There are four horses in *Zechariah 1:8-11*:

> In the night I saw a man riding on a red horse! He was standing among the myrtle trees in the glen; and behind him were red, sorrel, and white horses. Then I said, "What are these, my lord?" The angel who talked with me said to me, "I will show you what they are." So the man who was standing among the myrtle trees answered, "They are those whom the Lord has sent to patrol the earth." Then they spoke to the angel of the Lord who was standing among the myrtle trees, "We have patrolled the earth, and lo, the whole earth remains at peace."

In Zechariah, the role of these horses is somewhat ambiguous, but John brings clarity into their purpose. Zechariah could read the scroll only from the outside; John can read the inside.

In Zechariah's time these horsemen were wandering around the earth. It was the crucifixion and resurrection of Jesus that has released them to their purpose. The Lamb has opened the scroll and the horsemen wander no more but ride with purpose.

We can see how Revelation interprets the vision that Zechariah was unable to comprehend. Perceiving these four horsemen as being released as part of a coming end-time judgment is a hopelessly Western-centric view that does not consider the evidence of world history. But it is the opening of the scroll after Christ's death and resurrection in heaven that has released these four horsemen.

The evidence of world history is clear: these four horsemen have ridden the earth since the resurrection of the Lord, and the three other horsemen have been trying to ride past the white horseman bringing the good news. Even when the white horseman has ridden somewhere first, the destruction brought by the other three horsemen has always followed at the hoofs.

The horsemen never stay stationary; they are always on the move. One empire rises, another falls. What is constant is that war is always being waged somewhere, someone is always starving, pestilence always strikes somewhere. But the good news also is always advancing.

Humanity has already encountered many pestilences with the coronavirus epidemic spreading from 2020 onwards being a relatively

REVELATION 6

minor one. During the fourteenth century, the Black Death is estimated to have killed 30%-60% of Europe's population, reducing the world population from an estimated 450 million to 350-375 million. It would take two hundred years for the world population levels to recover after the plague had passed.

The Reformation was aided by the fact that many Europeans were expecting an imminent apocalypse because of world events, such as Vienna being sieged by the Muslims. In the Second World War around 60 million people lost their lives. In the Indonesian tsunami in 2004 nearly 170,000 lost their lives. This list could easily be continued by thousands of more examples.

So, the white horseman keeps on riding, and the three horsemen of destruction keep trying to catch him. This is very much in line with Jesus's prophecy in *Matthew 24:3-14*:

> When he was sitting on the Mount of Olives, the disciples came to him privately, saying, "Tell us, when will this be, and what will be the sign of your coming and of the end of the age?" Jesus answered them, "Beware that no one leads you astray. For many will come in my name, saying, 'I am the Messiah!' and they will lead many astray. And you will hear of wars and rumors of wars; see that you are not alarmed; for this must take place, but the end is not yet. For nation will rise against nation, and kingdom against kingdom, and there will be famines and earthquakes in various places: all this is but the beginning of the birth pangs. Then they will hand you over to be tortured and will put you to death, and you will be hated by all nations because of my name. Then many will fall away, and they will betray one another and hate one another. And many false prophets will arise and lead many astray. And because of the increase of lawlessness, the love of many will grow cold. But the one who endures to the end will be saved. And this good news of the kingdom will be proclaimed throughout the world, as a testimony to all the nations; and then the end will come."

Something different takes place when the Lamb opens the fifth seal. The martyrs who have been slain for the word of God and their testimony, asking for the judgment to come, "were each given a white robe and told to rest a little longer, until the number would be complete both of their fellow servants and of their brothers and sisters, who were soon to be killed as they themselves had been killed."

It is the cry of the martyrs that will compel the fifth seal to be opened. Again, seeing these martyrs only as end-time martyrs is a hopelessly Western-centric view. Through centuries, Christians have been martyred around the world. During the thirty-year genocide, between 1894 and 1924, three waves of violence swept across Anatolia, targeting the region's Christian minorities, who had previously accounted for 20% of the population. By 1924, the Armenians, Assyrians, and Greeks had been reduced to 2%. Over a million Armenians, Greeks and Assyrians were massacred during this time in what is now the modern Turkey, which is Asia Minor, where the seven churches of Revelation 2-3 were located. The gospel reached Asia Minor first, so that Asia Minor became the heartland of Christianity, but total devastation followed many years later.

The number of martyrs is closely linked to the advancement of the gospel. An increasing number of martyrs means an increasing number of saints. The destruction brought by the three horsemen affect the whole earth, but the fifth seal reveals the suffering inflicted, specifically on Christians.

Often, the persecution of Christians is part of a wider programme and can appear nearly accidental amidst other violence. In China today, Christians are persecuted, but so are the Muslims. In Pakistan, Christians are persecuted, but so are the Hindus. In India, Christians are persecuted, but so are the Muslims. In the Soviet Union, Christians were persecuted, but so were many other groups. But God knows every persecuted Christian and holds them in especially high regard.

When the Lamb opens the sixth seal, something changes. The sixth seal speeds to the final judgments, to the great day of the wrath of the Lamb when the kings of the earth try to hide from His wrath.

This is the first time in Revelation when the kings of the earth will understand that there will be a judgment that will come from the Lamb. But in *Revelation 9*, only a few chapters later, we are rewound to a time where the nations do not seem to understand that this is a judgment of God. This signals that the sixth seal indeed fast-forwards us to the end of time, but *Revelation 9* rewinds us back to an earlier time. There is a temporal overlap between two different visions.

REVELATION 6

The scroll cannot be unrolled fully until the seventh seal has been broken. But we are already glimpsing on what the opening of the seventh seal might mean. The scroll is nearly fully open, and we can read it nearly to the end.

The fifth seal reveals something that will take place in heaven because of the martyrs, whereas the sixth seal reveals the consequences of the judgment on earth because of the blood of the martyrs.

The opening of the sixth seal means that whoever will be on earth at the time will be experiencing the end-time judgments that will be released on the earth because of the sufferings of the martyrs. But the opening of the sixth seal begins to release them. The end-time judgments are now fully activated.

It is important to understand that the earth is being punished because of the blood of the martyrs. That would mean that what many name as "born-again" Christians no more inhabit the earth.

Isaiah 29:6-7 foretells:

> You will be visited by the Lord of hosts with thunder and earthquake and great noise, with whirlwind and tempest, and the flame of a devouring fire. And the multitude of all the nations that fight against Ariel, all that fight against her and her stronghold, and who distress her, shall be like a dream, a vision of the night.

Ezekiel 38:19-21 prophesies:

> For in my jealousy and in my blazing wrath I declare: On that day there shall be a great shaking in the land of Israel; the fish of the sea, and the birds of the air, and the animals of the field, and all creeping things that creep on the ground, and all human beings that are on the face of the earth, shall quake at my presence, and the mountains shall be thrown down, and the cliffs shall fall, and every wall shall tumble to the ground. I will summon the sword against Gog in all my mountains, says the Lord God; the swords of all will be against their comrades.

The sixth seal begins to release an end-time war that has not yet taken place. We can see how the end-time Israel revealed to us in *Revelation*

UNDERSTANDING REVELATION

1 via hyperlinks to the Old Testament prophecies now returns to focus. For a while, the Church will not be the focal point, but Israel.

Isaiah 34:1-4 prophesies:

> Draw near, O nations, to hear; O peoples, give heed! Let the earth hear, and all that fills it; the world, and all that comes from it. For the Lord is enraged against all the nations, and furious against all their hordes; he has doomed them, has given them over for slaughter. Their slain shall be cast out, and the stench of their corpses shall rise; the mountains shall flow with their blood. All the host of heaven shall rot away, and the skies roll up like a scroll. All their host shall wither like a leaf withering on a vine, or fruit withering on a fig tree.

All these Old Testament prophecies refer to God's wrath in the end of times. Nearly every Old Testament prophet prophesied about the great day of the Lord's wrath, when He would judge the nations.

So, *Revelation 6* fast-forwards to the end, to the time when the Church is no more the focal point of God's plan on earth. We see that in the beginning of *Revelation 7*, which focuses on the elect of Israel.

As we have seen, Revelation is a series of vision, and there can be temporal gaps and overlaps between these visions. One vision goes quickly to the end without explaining everything, but the following visions will explain the gaps left in the previous visions. So, by the opening of the sixth seal the end is clearly in sight, but what will happen before the end has not yet been fully explained.

Perhaps this way of telling has something to do with the limits of visual language. A film can explore only one central idea; exploring a multitude of them would only bring confusion. The same applies to the written narrative; it is impossible to expand on a multitude of concepts through a singular narrative without creating confusion.

The Third Vision

REVELATION 7

Revelation 7 continues the story in *Revelation 6*. It is still the day of God's wrath in the end-times. But as it begins with "After this", and the change of perspective is drastic, it should be approached as a separate vision.

In *verse 1*, four angels stop all the winds on the earth. These four angels have been given power to harm the land and the sea. But there is a time of waiting, until the 144,000 have been sealed.

Much has been written about these 144,000, and many elitist doctrines have been formulated around them. For example, the Jehovah Witnesses believe that only the 144,000 will ever make it to heaven, with the rest of the saints remaining on earth.

What does the number 144,000 stand for? Clearly, it represents the Jews that have been saved, especially as the tribal list with an exact number is contrasted with a vision of a great multitude from all nations, too many to number.

The number of tribes, twelve, is an idealistic number, as there were in fact thirteen tribes but only twelve sons of Jacob, who had been renamed Israel by God. And this ideal number of twelve is reached in different ways in the Bible. There were thirteen tribes, because Joseph had two sons, Ephraim and Manasseh, and both of their descendants were numbered with the tribes.

The list of Jacob's sons is mentioned in *Genesis 29-30*. But in the tribal census recorded in *Numbers 1*, Levi is missing, which creates a space to list both sons of Joseph. Had Levi been included, there would have been thirteen tribes. The theological justification for not listing Levi here is that Levi had been dedicated to the Lord to be

UNDERSTANDING REVELATION

a tribe of priests, and God asked not to count the Levites in Israel's army.

But, in the list of twelve tribes in *Revelation 7*, Levi is back. The Second Temple has been destroyed, and there is no need for the Levitical priesthood. In fact, every tribe is like Levi—a tribe of priests.

But Dan is missing from the list. Why did the list miss Dan? According to *Judges 18*, the tribe of Dan brought idolatry to Israel. In *Revelation 14*, the 144,000 are referred to as virgins. The exclusion of Dan seems to imply the absence of spiritual adultery; unlike the prostitute Church in Revelation 17, these 144,000 Jews have not compromised their devotion to God.

These 144,000 remain on earth when the multitude of nations are standing in front of the Lamb's throne. The true Church of God has been raptured to heaven, and out of the elect, only Israel remains on earth for the final tribulation.

The nations are multitudes, but the number of Jews with the seal of God is much smaller. It appears that John does not expect the restoration of the Levitical priesthood in the end-times. Also, this 144,000 is a remnant and a symbolic number; even when many Jews have rejected the gospel, God will still have His chosen ones amongst them.

Verses 9-17 give a picture of the saints' heavenly destination and eternal joy. They are a multitude that no one can count. John is clearly expecting a great harvest of souls to come to faith. This is a significant prophecy, especially as in the time of writing, most Christian communities would have been quite small.

Paul says it slightly differently in *Ephesians 2:11-18*:

> So then, remember that at one time you Gentiles by birth, called "the uncircumcision" by those who are called "the circumcision"—a physical circumcision made in the flesh by human hands—remember that you were at that time without Christ, being aliens from the commonwealth of Israel, and strangers to the covenants of promise, having no hope and without God in the world. But now in Christ Jesus you who once were far off have been brought near by the blood of Christ. For he is our peace; in his flesh he has made both groups into one and has broken down the dividing wall, that is, the hostility

REVELATION 7

between us. He has abolished the law with its commandments and ordinances, that he might create in himself one new humanity in place of the two, thus making peace, and might reconcile both groups to God in one body through the cross, thus putting to death that hostility through it. So he came and proclaimed peace to you who were far off and peace to those who were near; for through him both of us have access in one Spirit to the Father.

Revelation 7 is placed between the sixth and seventh seals, but it does not follow the sixth seal in a chronological and linear succession. Instead, it presents the outcome of the releasing of the four horsemen and the opening of the four first seals, and the purpose of world history from the heavenly perspective.

All events that have taken place will happen so that there will be a great harvest of souls from Israel and the nations. And now, the whole harvest from the nations has been gathered, whereas some of the harvest from Israel remains on earth.

The Fourth Vision

REVELATION 8

The sixth seal and the seventh seal are the seals that bring focus on the final judgments of the end-times. *Revelation 8* continues from where the opening of the sixth seal in *Revelation 6* left us—the third vision about the 144,000 and the multitudes has been inserted between the sixth and the seventh seal to give us the heavenly perspective about the purpose of world history and to indicate that those who have followed Jesus are already in heaven, whereas some of the ones destined to be redeemed from Israel are still on earth. Accepting Christ has saved believers from the coming wrath. But this implies that these end-time Jews represented by the 144,000 here are yet to accept Christ as their Messiah.

When the seventh seal is broken, there is a silence in heaven that lasts for about half an hour. This indicates that there is one final delay before the final end-time judgments will begin. This half an hour is time of heaven, which is the time zone of eternity, so we do not quite know how long this silence will last on earth.

This silence might mean various things. But it clearly means that God is not taking these judgments lightly. Perhaps heaven is silent because of the deep sorrow in God's heart for what is about to happen. A series of destructive events is about to be set in motion. And there are no words to describe them. If there was a way to delay or annul this judgment, God would do it. But these final judgments must be released.

The seven angels, who stand before God, are given seven trumpets. Another angel receives much incense from the altar in front of the throne. This incense represents the prayers of the saints and the blood of the martyrs. Then the angel takes the censer, fills it with fire from the altar and hurls it on the earth.

This means that the end-time judgments will be released because of the prayers of the saints and because of the martyrs.

The vision about the sixth seal in *Revelation 6* had fast-forwarded to the final judgment in all its fullness and explained the wrath of the Lamb as the fulfilment of the Old Testament prophecies.

This vision begins to outline what God's wrath will look like:

> The first angel sounds the trumpet, and hail and fire are hurled down to the earth. A third of the earth is burned up.

The second angel blows a trumpet, and something like a huge mountain, all ablaze, is thrown at sea. A third of the sea is destroyed with ships included.

The third angel sounds his trumpet, and a great star, blazing like a torch, falls on the sky on third of the rivers and on the springs of water.

The fourth angel sounds his trumpet, and a third of the sun, third of the stars and third of the moon turn dark.

Taken together, this begins to look something like the consequences of a nuclear holocaust. It might not be, but that is what it looks like. And it would be the fitting finale for humanity's rebellion to end in self-destruction.

Even Buddhism and Hinduism recognise the biblical principle of sowing and reaping. They call it karma, but they connect it to a false metaphysical and religious framework. This is the moment when humanity will begin to reap in fullness from the sins they have sown.

These might not be individual plagues but part of the same series of catastrophic events.

It is difficult to convey simultaneity within a written narrative, but it is a lot easier to write it down in sequence. Equally, had John seen all these events as one image, it would have probably been overpoweringly confusing.

Some say that the judgments of God on earth should be supernatural. But that does not need to be the case. The judgment of God is to remove His grace, and after that, we will reap the consequences of our wickedness.

REVELATION 8

Jesus says in *Matthew 5:44-45*:

> But I say to you, love your enemies and pray for those who persecute you, so that you may be children of your Father in heaven; for he makes his sun rise on the evil and on the good, and sends rain on the righteous and on the unrighteous.

In the time of grace God lets His blessings shine on everyone. But the time of grace is now over. Romans *1:18-19* says:

> For the wrath of God is revealed from heaven against all ungodliness and wickedness of those who by their wickedness suppress the truth. For what can be known about God is plain to them, because God has shown it to them.

How is this wrath of God revealed? *Verse 24* provides us with the answer: "Therefore God gave them up in the lusts of their hearts to impurity, to the degrading of their bodies among themselves".

God's wrath is to give men up to their sins. We have already created the arsenal of weapons for our own destruction. Perhaps God will simply allow us to use them. There were many moments during the Cold War when a nuclear holocaust was nearly released on earth because of confusion and misunderstandings. But God's grace stopped it from happening each time.

In Paul's understanding, the wrath of God means that He lets humanity reap what it has sown. God stops interfering in the affairs of men. And the consequences will be devastating.

When I was a young man, I heard a warning prophecy at a Christian youth conference. The prophecy was given publicly to the whole conference, and as a result, many young people responded by going to the altar. According to the prophecy, there was a young man in the conference, and unless he repented from his ways, God would remove His protection from his life for a moment.

My friend told me some months later that he knew that he was the person that the prophecy had been addressed to, but that he would not change his behaviour. He was ready to suffer the consequences. Two weeks later he had a terrible accident, and he is still partially paralysed decades later.

UNDERSTANDING REVELATION

God removed His protection for a moment, and my friend reaped the fruit of his actions. But only a few seconds later He reinstated His protection, and my friend lived. I do not think that the end-time judgments are anything more than that. We have the capacity to destroy human life on earth many times over. Perhaps, one day, all it takes is that God allows one finger press a button.

Through history, most judgments of God on a nation have been delivered by other nations. Israel was always judged with onslaughts by other nations. This time, the whole humanity is under judgment.

In the earlier stages of world history, when the four horsemen were riding, the judgments were more limited. Now they expand in scale.

The judgments brought by the last three trumpets are different in nature from the first four. They release the full power of the demonic dimension on earth. But they are part of the same judgment, only they reveal that this judgment is brought by God allowing the demonic forces to operate freely.

When Adam and Eve ate the fruit offered by the snake, or Lucifer, the cherub guarding the paradise, it brought a limited judgment on man. But God still protected humanity from the full exposure to satanic powers. But now the demonic forces are released on earth without restraint.

Until this moment, the interaction between humanity and the demonic realm has been restricted. In Paradise, man was able to converse both with God and the snake. The man chose to listen to the snake; now he has been left on earth with the snake he listened to. And it turns out that the snake is a dragon! But those who chose to listen to God have been taken up to Him. Now the snake and humanity can coexist without hindrance. But this can only bring destruction.

The wrath of God can only be released after the gospel has been preached to all nations. Every nation must be given the chance to accept or reject the gospel before they will be judged.

REVELATION 9

Revelation 9 begins with the fifth angel sounding the fifth trumpet. John sees a star that had fallen from the sky to the earth. We do not know exactly when the star had fallen, only that its fall has already taken place.

Revelation 9 continues the account of sounding the seven trumpets. But there is a crucial difference between the first four and the last three trumpets of judgment. The first four focus on the physical dimension, the remaining three on its spiritual dimension.

This fallen star is either Lucifer or another high-ranking fallen angel. He is given the key to the Abyss. The smoke rising from the Abyss darkens the sky and the sun. Out come locusts, which are given power like of scorpions. These locusts are told not to harm the grass, any plant or tree, but only those people who do not have the seal of God on their foreheads. They torture them for five months. Because of the pain, people seek death, but in vain.

John gives a vivid description about the physical appearance of these locusts, but it is enough to know that their king is the demon of the Abyss, *Abaddon* (Hebrew), *Apollyon* (Greek)—the destroyer—to understand that they are a demonic army.

The duration of five months might appear perplexing, but the most likely reference point is *Genesis 7:24*, which says:

> And the waters swelled on the earth for one hundred fifty days.

This was the aftermath of the Flood. After it had rained for forty days with Noah and his family in the safety of the ark, it took five months

UNDERSTANDING REVELATION

for the water to recede. So, these five months are the aftermath of judgment.

Genesis 7:1 says:

> Then the Lord said to Noah, "Go into the ark, you and all your household, for I have seen that you alone are righteous before me in this generation."

It seems clear that all the believers, apart from the sealed of Israel, will be in the ark of salvation and saved from these plagues.

Genesis 6:13 says:

> And God said to Noah, "I have determined to make an end of all flesh, for the earth is filled with violence because of them; now I am going to destroy them along with the earth."

God promised Noah that He would never again destroy the world with water. But He did not mention fire. As the five months stands for the receding of waters, the last three trumpets could signify the aftermath of the destruction caused by the first four trumpets.

This is a clear reference to the Day of the Lord in the Book of Joel. *Joel 2:1-11* says:

> Blow the trumpet in Zion; sound the alarm on my holy mountain! Let all the inhabitants of the land tremble, for the day of the Lord is coming, it is near—a day of darkness and gloom, a day of clouds and thick darkness! Like blackness spread upon the mountains a great and powerful army comes; their like has never been from of old, nor will be again after them in ages to come. Fire devours in front of them, and behind them a flame burns. Before them the land is like the garden of Eden, but after them a desolate wilderness, and nothing escapes them. They have the appearance of horses, and like war-horses they charge. As with the rumbling of chariots, they leap on the tops of the mountains, like the crackling of a flame of fire devouring the stubble, like a powerful army drawn up for battle. Before them peoples are in anguish, all faces grow pale. Like warriors they charge, like soldiers they scale the wall. Each keeps to its own course, they do not swerve from their

REVELATION 9

> paths. They do not jostle one another, each keeps to its own track; they burst through the weapons and are not halted. They leap upon the city, they run upon the walls; they climb up into the houses, they enter through the windows like a thief. The earth quakes before them, the heavens tremble. The sun and the moon are darkened, and the stars withdraw their shining. The Lord utters his voice at the head of his army; how vast is his host! Numberless are those who obey his command. Truly the day of the Lord is great; terrible indeed—who can endure it?

Revelation reinterprets Joel's prophecy and adds to it. The physical army has now become demonic. This is fitting, as all humanity is now under God's judgment. There is no conquering army left that is not under judgment. Any further judgment must be sourced from the demonic world, as their judgment still awaits.

Humanity will finally taste the full consequences of what it means to side with Satan.

Until now, the key to the Abyss has been with Jesus. The demons captured in the Abyss have remained imprisoned there. In *Matthew 8:28-34*, the demons are frightened that Jesus would cast them into the Abyss, so they beg that Jesus would send them to the pigs instead. Now the gates of the Abyss are opened wide, and any demons that have been tormented "before time" are freed. This demonic presence will be severe and have devastating consequences. Because the saved are in the ark, the demons are not given many restrictions.

Many years ago, I met a woman who was demon-possessed. She was a cult priestess, and when she came to contact with our evangelism team, the demonic beings controlling her manifested so violently that her face became distorted as if it were an animal's face. You could glimpse into the darkness through her eyes.

She told us that demons were tormenting her. She had invited them in, but now they were destroying her soul. She wanted for the torment to go but keep the demonic power. But that is not possible.

Even when this woman had devoted herself to Satan, the demonic presence was still torment. Most people are deaf and blind to the presence of demons. But their unobstructed presence is extremely uncomfortable.

UNDERSTANDING REVELATION

These sufferings will have a physical dimension, but their origin will be demonic. What is unclear is if mankind will perceive their origin to be demonic or natural.

Then the sixth angel sounds the trumpet and releases the four angels that have been bound at the river Euphrates. These four angels have two hundred million demons at their command.

What does it mean that these demons have been bound? It seems that the Abyss has already been emptied, but that for some reason, a great demonic army has been bound at the river Euphrates, which runs through Turkey, Syria, Iraq, Iran, Kuwait, and Saudi Arabia. This implies that their activity has been limited to this area.

A third of humanity is killed by the release of this demonic army because of the plagues of fire, smoke and sulphur that come out of their mouths. As a third of the world has already been destroyed by the four first trumpets, it is likely that the fifth and the sixth trumpet describe the human cost of this same destruction.

Sulphur is an ingredient of crude oil, and the oil fields of the Middle East were known thousands of years ago for their burning that could last for years.

This is a demonic army, but the location of this army must have significance. Unfortunately, there are not any Old Testament references to these demons.

It is difficult to say what the timeline is, but as I have said, it seems that these six trumpets might refer to the same catastrophic events. So, even when they seem to follow a chronological sequence, that might not necessarily be the case. They might also be simultaneous or overlapping.

Genesis 2:10-14 says:

> A river flows out of Eden to water the garden, and from there it divides and becomes four branches. The name of the first is Pishon; it is the one that flows around the whole land of Havilah, where there is gold; and the gold of that land is good; bdellium and onyx stone are there. The name of the second river is Gihon; it is the one that flows around the whole land of Cush. The name of the third river is Tigris, which flows east of Assyria. And the fourth river is the Euphrates.

REVELATION 9

The Euphrates takes us back to Eden. These four demons, perhaps connected to the four rivers streaming out of Eden, will be releasing the judgment that God has delayed since the time of Adam and Eve.

In Genesis, there are six days of creation, In Revelation, there are six trumpets of judgment.

After the first trumpet, a third of the earth was burned up, a third of the trees were burned up and all the green grass was burned up. After the second trumpet, a third of the sea was burned into blood and third of the living creatures in the sea died. After the third trumpet, a third of the waters turned bitter, after the fourth trumpet a third of the sun, moon and stars were darkened, after the fifth trumpet the people suffered for five months, and after the sixth trumpet a third of the mankind were killed with the destruction originating from the area around Eden.

No death of animals apart from sea creatures is mentioned in the list, but this seems like God's judgment on the creation because of man's sin. In *Genesis 1*, God creates life on earth, in *Revelation 8-9*, He releases the curse that He has delayed because of His mercy.

On the seventh day of creation God rested; the seventh trumpet will bring the final rest of God's eternal Kingdom.

Revelation 9:20 says that the rest of the mankind did not repent or stop worshiping demons. In *Revelation 6:15-17*, people understand that it is the wrath of God and they try to hide from it, but later in Revelation 9, the people still do not understand that this is the wrath of the Lamb.

This must mean that, chronologically, *Revelation 6:15-17* will take place later in future than *Revelation 8-9*. In Revelation, there are flash-forwards and flashbacks, much like in movies.

Revelation 6:15-17 refers to the prophecy in *Isaiah 2:19-21*:

> Enter the caves of the rocks and the holes of the ground, from the terror of the Lord, and from the glory of his majesty, when he rises to terrify the earth. On that day people will throw away to the moles and to the bats their idols of silver and their idols of gold, which they made for themselves to worship, to enter the caverns of the rocks and the clefts in the crags, from the terror of the Lord, and from the glory of his majesty, when he rises to terrify the earth.

UNDERSTANDING REVELATION

Also, it makes a reference to *Zephaniah 1:14-15*:

> The great day of the Lord is near, near and hastening fast; the sound of the day of the Lord is bitter, the warrior cries aloud there. That day will be a day of wrath, a day of distress and anguish, a day of ruin and devastation, a day of darkness and gloom, a day of clouds and thick darkness.

So, the final verses of *Revelation 6* rush to the end, but *Revelation 8-9* winds back and accounts what will take place more slowly.

The Fifth Vision

REVELATION 10

Another mighty angel with the voices of seven thunders roars like a lion. The rainbow over his head is a reference to the covenant between God and all life on earth established in *Genesis 9*. There will never be another earth-destroying flood, but the angel's legs which are like pillars of fire imply what will be in store for the earth.

John is about to write down what the thunder says, but God's voice stops him. Some things must remain secrets.

Yet, John can hear the words of thunder. But he is not allowed to share them. Why?

There might be multiple reasons for that. But often God speaks to prophets and gives them additional knowledge as release notes. This will help a prophet to share the prophecy accurately. But sharing these notes might not be useful.

The angel promises there will be no more delay. At the time of the blowing of the seventh trumpet the mystery of God will be accomplished. The seventh day of creation accomplished the fullness of God's blessing on earth. The seventh trumpet will accomplish the fullness of God's plan on earth.

The angel has a little scroll that he asks John to eat. Rather than allowing John to share what the thunder said, God gives him another prophecy.

John hears in *verse 11*:

> You must prophesy again about many peoples, nations, tongues, and kings.

UNDERSTANDING REVELATION

The scroll tastes like sweet honey in John's mouth, but his stomach turns sour.

This is a vital clue. The little scroll indicates a new prophecy, a small prophecy, a prophecy about something else than what has been shared before.

This is a reference to *Ezekiel 3:1-9*:

> He said to me, "O mortal, eat what is offered to you; eat this scroll, and go, speak to the house of Israel." So I opened my mouth, and he gave me the scroll to eat. He said to me, "Mortal, eat this scroll that I give you and fill your stomach with it." Then I ate it; and in my mouth it was as sweet as honey. He said to me: "Mortal, go to the house of Israel and speak my very words to them. For you are not sent to a people of obscure speech and difficult language, but to the house of Israel—not to many peoples of obscure speech and difficult language, whose words you cannot understand. Surely, if I sent you to them, they would listen to you. But the house of Israel will not listen to you, for they are not willing to listen to me; because all the house of Israel have a hard forehead and a stubborn heart. See, I have made your face hard against their faces, and your forehead hard against their foreheads. Like the hardest stone, harder than flint, I have made your forehead; do not fear them or be dismayed at their looks, for they are a rebellious house."

The small scroll begins a prophecy for Israel. The large scroll covers the whole world. The small scroll covers Israel. So, *Revelation 11* takes us back to Jerusalem.

The Sixth Vision

REVELATION 11

The small scroll prophecy begins with John given a reed like a measuring rod. John is told to measure the temple of God, but to exclude the outer court, because the Gentiles would trample on the holy city for 42 months—the time of three and a half years.

God would give power to His two witnesses who would prophesy for 1,260 days—also three and a half years.

The obvious reference point in the Old Testament is the vision about the new temple that begins in *Ezekiel 40* with a man measuring the temple. Ezekiel sees the vision in the twenty-fifth year of his exile and in the fourteenth year after the fall of the Jerusalem.

This temple of Ezekiel has never been built, which has led many to believe that there will once be an end-time physical temple like it. The Second Temple was built according to a different kind of pattern; it did not follow Ezekiel's pattern.

Ezekiel 43:10-11 gives us an important clue:

> As for you, mortal, describe the temple to the house of Israel, and let them measure the pattern; and let them be ashamed of their iniquities. When they are ashamed of all that they have done, make known to them the plan of the temple, its arrangement, its exits and its entrances, and its whole form—all its ordinances and its entire plan and all its laws; and write it down in their sight, so that they may observe and follow the entire plan and all its ordinances.

UNDERSTANDING REVELATION

This temple of Ezekiel is a challenge and a judgment for the people of Israel. It is what Israel could have built had they truly repented. It is an ideal model.

In *Zechariah 2*, another man is on his way to measure Jerusalem.

Both Ezekiel and Zechariah see someone else doing the measuring. But in John's vision it is John himself who is measuring the temple. The indications are clear: both Zechariah and Ezekiel are prophesying about a future event; one day someone will measure. John is measuring the temple himself; it is taking place in his time.

In fact, the measuring had already happened. Jerusalem had already been measured for judgment. Jesus had prophesied about that. And it had already fallen. The little scroll is both an explanation and a prophecy.

This is a similar vision than the one about the four horsemen that had not yet been released in *Zechariah* 1, whereas they were roaming free in *Revelation 6*.

The little scroll accounts for the destruction of the Second Temple and the coming restoration of Israel.

Many eschatologists see the two witnesses as two end-time human beings who will be miraculously resurrected after lying dead on the streets of Jerusalem. And the fact that they can be seen by all the nations is taken as evidence that this is an end-time event, as TV and Internet would make it possible.

But who are these two witnesses, really? To explain this, we need to begin from the Bible itself and follow the principles of interpretation Revelation itself gives to us. First, the two witnesses are a clear reference to *Zechariah 4:14*:

> These are the two anointed ones who stand by the Lord of the whole earth.

These anointed ones in Zechariah's vision are two olive trees standing by one lampstand with seven lights, Joshua the High Priest, and Zerubbabel, the civil ruler, who were tasked with laying the physical and spiritual foundations of the Second Temple.

But Joshua the High Priest and Zerubbabel are not described as witnesses in Zechariah. So, there must be more. And there

REVELATION 11

have always been two clear witnesses in Israel: the Law and the Prophets.

In *Luke 16:29*, in Jesus's parable about the rich man and Lazarus in the afterlife, when the rich man is begging Abraham to send Lazarus to speak to his brothers so that they would repent, Abraham replies:

> They have Moses and the prophets; they should listen to them.

The two witnesses of *Revelation 11* are the Law and the Prophets. This is made abundantly clear, as these two witnesses have the power of Moses and Elijah. Moses could turn the waters into blood and strike the earth with every kind of plague, whereas Elijah could stop the rain. Moses represents the Law and Elijah represents the Prophets. The two witnesses are taken to heaven in a cloud, as their enemies look on. Elijah was taken to heaven in a cloud; the Bible is not clear about what happened to Moses's body.

The loud voice from heaven tells the two witnesses to come up, and they ascend to heaven in a cloud. This is a clear reference to the Transfiguration, where Moses and Elijah first appear and then disappear. Matthew *17:1-8* says:

> Six days later, Jesus took with him Peter and James and his brother John and led them up a high mountain, by themselves. And he was transfigured before them, and his face shone like the sun, and his clothes became dazzling white. Suddenly there appeared to them Moses and Elijah, talking with him. Then Peter said to Jesus, "Lord, it is good for us to be here; if you wish, I will make three dwellings here, one for you, one for Moses, and one for Elijah." While he was still speaking, suddenly a bright cloud overshadowed them, and from the cloud a voice said, "This is my Son, the Beloved; with him I am well pleased; listen to him!" When the disciples heard this, they fell to the ground and were overcome by fear. But Jesus came and touched them, saying, "Get up and do not be afraid." And when they looked up, they saw no one except Jesus himself alone.

At the Transfiguration both the Law and the Prophets testified for Jesus.

UNDERSTANDING REVELATION

In this vision of *Revelation 11*, Moses and Elijah, and Joshua the High Priest and Zerubbabel, are merged into one vision.

It was Joshua the High Priest and Zerubbabel who were instrumental in building the Second Temple, which had been destroyed in John's time, because the Law and the Prophets had testified against it.

That they are dead signifies that the physical Israel centred on Jerusalem is dead. Their resurrection means that the physical Israel would be resurrected one day. They are in sackcloth, which was used for mourning and repentance.

Luke 19:41-44 says about Jesus:

> As he came near and saw the city, he wept over it, saying, "If you, even you, had only recognized on this day the things that make for peace! But now they are hidden from your eyes. Indeed, the days will come upon you, when your enemies will set up ramparts around you and surround you, and hem you in on every side. They will crush you to the ground, you and your children within you, and they will not leave within you one stone upon another; because you did not recognize the time of your visitation from God."

Jesus prophesied about the destruction of Jerusalem during the First Jewish-Roman War in AD 66-73, over thirty years before it took place.

So, the two witnesses are the Law and the Prophets, and they are testifying *against* Jerusalem. Only after their resurrection they will be testifying to the world, and according to *verse 11*, great fear will fall on those who see them resurrected. Three and a half years signifies drought in Israel. Jesus said in *Luke 4:25*:

> But the truth is, there were many widows in Israel in the time of Elijah, when the heaven was shut up three years and six months, and there was a severe famine over all the land.

This drought came as judgment in times of Elijah. What is the judgment in Revelation? The Gentiles will trample over the holy city for forty-two months—the symbolic time for God's prophetic

REVELATION 11

judgment. Yet, these two witnesses are *also* olive trees and lampstands. What does that mean?

The state symbol of the modern Israel is two olive tree branches and a Menorah. The olive trees and lampstands stand for Israel.

There are no seven years of tribulation divided in two halves, as many eschatologists would explain it. These are not literal years but Israel's drought, which is divided in two parts with the first part the oppression of Israel after returning from the exile in Babylon and the second part the time after the destruction of the Second Temple until the birth of the modern Israel. Jesus says in *Matthew 5:17*:

> Do not think that I came to destroy the Law or the Prophets. I did not come to destroy but to fulfill.

What happened after Jesus fulfilled the Law and the Prophets? *Mark 13:1-2* says:

> As he came out of the temple, one of his disciples said to him, "Look, Teacher, what large stones and what large buildings!" Then Jesus asked him, "Do you see these great buildings? Not one stone will be left here upon another; all will be thrown down."

The destruction of Jerusalem and the Second Temple was a visible sign of the end of the Old Covenant and the fact that Jesus had fulfilled the Law and the Prophets.

When the Law and the Prophets have finished their testimony, a beast is released from hell and overcomes them. John says that their dead bodies will lie in the street of the city, which spiritually is called Sodom and Egypt—the city where Jesus was crucified. Both Sodom and Egypt were judged, which means that Jerusalem has also been judged. Their bodies are not allowed to be buried. After the drought is over, they will be resurrected—as the modern Israel.

This means that although the nation of Israel has been destroyed and looks dead, this is not the end. Israel is slain but not buried. In the meantime, the nations will celebrate Israel's demise.

If you visit Rome, you can still see the Arch of Titus, which was constructed by Emperor Domitian in AD 82 to commemorate his

UNDERSTANDING REVELATION

older brother's victories, including the siege of Jerusalem. This arch has provided the model for many triumphal arches erected since the sixteenth century. The Menorah depicted on it was used as a model for the Menorah on the emblem of the state of Israel, with the symbol of shame transformed into the symbol of victory.

After the three and a half days, the breath of life from God entered the two witnesses, and great fear fell on those who see them. The resurrection of the state of Israel is one of the modern-day miracles.

These few verses are so full of references to the Old Testament that it can be easy to miss some of them. For example, Zerubbabel, one of the two olive trees, led the first group of Jews, numbering 42,360, who returned from the Babylonian captivity in the first year of Cyrus, King of Persia.

So, like Zerubbabel who led the first group of Jews from the exile, one day a group of Jews would return to Israel. This would be the resurrection of one of the two witnesses. But Zerubbabel was not a king but merely a governor. This indicates that this is not the restoration of Israel as a priestly kingdom.

The reference to the second olive tree, Joshua the High Priest, does leave some options open. Will there be a restoration of the temple cult? To me, it is more likely that this means that the Jewish people will one day discover Jesus, the High Priest.

This is followed by a severe earthquake with one tenth of Jerusalem collapsing and seven thousand people being killed in the earthquake. The survivors—the Jews in Jerusalem—are terrified but give glory to God. *Zechariah 14:1-5* says:

> See, a day is coming for the Lord, when the plunder taken from you will be divided in your midst. For I will gather all the nations against Jerusalem to battle, and the city shall be taken and the houses looted and the women raped; half the city shall go into exile, but the rest of the people shall not be cut off from the city. Then the Lord will go forth and fight against those nations as when he fights on a day of battle. On that day his feet shall stand on the Mount of Olives, which lies before Jerusalem on the east; and the Mount of Olives shall be split in two from east to west by a very wide valley; so that one half of the Mount shall withdraw northward, and the other half southward. And

REVELATION 11

> you shall flee by the valley of the Lord's mountain, for the valley between the mountains shall reach to Azal; and you shall flee as you fled from the earthquake in the days of King Uzziah of Judah. Then the Lord my God will come, and all the holy ones with him.

Suddenly, this vision in Revelation speeds to the end, as after the sounding of the seventh trumpet, *verse 15* says:

> The kingdom of the world has become the kingdom of our Lord and of his Messiah, and he will reign forever and ever.

The seventh trumpet brings the Kingdom of God—this is the END. Most visions in Revelation begin either from the time of Jesus's birth, resurrection, or the destruction of the Second Temple, and they select different events in time that are vital to that narrative, before they culminate in the end of days.

Verse 19 says:

> Then God's temple in heaven was opened, and the ark of his covenant was seen within his temple; and there were flashes of lightning, rumblings, peals of thunder, an earthquake, and heavy hail.

The ark of the covenant in heaven reinforces the idea that this message is related to Israel. God will once more remember His covenant with Israel. The temple of God is in heaven and not on earth, which implies that the restoration of the temple cult might not take place. After the Lamb has been slain, there is no need for the restoration of an earthly temple building in Jerusalem. There is no need for more animal sacrifices. But there remains a need for the Jews to discover that they once missed their Messiah.

In summary, the opening of the little scroll takes us back to seeing the world history from Israel's perspective. The two witnesses—the Law and the Prophets, proclaim judgment against Israel for three and a half years. This is the time of the oppression of Israel under foreign powers until the destruction of the Second Temple. They lay dead for three and a half years, until they are resurrected. This is the time between the destruction of the Second Temple and the birth of the modern Israel.

The seventh angel blows the trumpet, which brings together the developments in the fourth and the sixth vision with the fifth vision not being revealed to us.

The end of the chapter takes us to the time of judging the dead, which indicates that we have arrived in the end of times.

The Seventh Vision

REVELATION 12

Revelation 11 ends with the beginning of the reign of the Lord. *Revelation 12* takes us back to the birth of Jesus. Now the focus is both on Israel and the Church.

A woman clothed with the sun, with the moon under her feet and twelve stars on her head, is pregnant. She cries out in pain, as she is about to give birth. This woman is a reference to Israel, as *Genesis 37:9-11* says about Joseph:

> He had another dream, and told it to his brothers, saying, "Look, I have had another dream: the sun, the moon, and eleven stars were bowing down to me." But when he told it to his father and to his brothers, his father rebuked him, and said to him, "What kind of dream is this that you have had? Shall we indeed come, I and your mother and your brothers, and bow to the ground before you?" So his brothers were jealous of him, but his father kept the matter in mind.

In Joseph's dream the eleven stars represent the eleven other sons of Jacob, the sun their father Jacob, and the moon Joseph's mother.

This woman is Israel, as he is dressed with Jacob and his wife Rachel, and with the twelve sons of Jacob—Israel.

Then another sign appears in heaven; an enormous dragon with seven heads, ten horns and seven crowns, stands in front of the woman to devour her child—a son who will rule all nations with an iron sceptre.

This dragon has a third of the stars following him; he is the devil and one third of the angels have followed him in rebellion against

UNDERSTANDING REVELATION

God. But the dragon is nearly fully identified with the Roman Empire. We will look at this in more detail in the next chapter, but, for now, it is enough to say that this is continuation of the prophecy in *Daniel 7*, which, quite remarkably, connects with Revelation through an accurate description of the year AD 69, which was the Year of the Four Emperors in the Roman Empire. Daniel's prophecy about the three kings replaced by one king is one of the most remarkable prophecies in the Bible.

The child is snatched up to God and to His throne. Here we have an image similar than the Lamb coming to the throne in Revelation 5. So, we learn that the Lamb who appeared in heaven is also the Child.

Isaiah 9:6-7 prophesies:

> For a child has been born for us, a son given to us; authority rests upon his shoulders; and he is named Wonderful Counselor, Mighty God, Everlasting Father, Prince of Peace. His authority shall grow continually, and there shall be endless peace for the throne of David and his kingdom. He will establish and uphold it with justice and with righteousness from this time onward and forevermore. The zeal of the Lord of hosts will do this.

The symbolism is made crystal-clear. The Child is also God. But He is also the Messiah.

After that, the woman flees into the desert, where she will be taken care of for 1,260 days. This is yet another reference to three and a half years. If we accept that the woman is Israel, which she must be, as she gives birth to Jesus, then these 1,260 days must refer to the exile of the Jews who are now in the wilderness and stateless.

This is the time of Israel's drought when heaven will be shut for Israel as a nation, hence she will be in the wilderness. But she will also be protected by God.

We can see again how the 1,260 days or three and a half years work in Revelation not as a precise number but to mark spiritual drought or separation from God.

In *verse 7*, there is a war in heaven, and the dragon and his angels lose their place there. The great dragon—Satan—is hurled to the earth, and his angels with him. *Verses 10-12* say:

REVELATION 12

> Then I heard a loud voice in heaven, proclaiming, "Now have come the salvation and the power and the kingdom of our God and the authority of his Messiah, for the accuser of our comrades has been thrown down, who accuses them day and night before our God. But they have conquered him by the blood of the Lamb and by the word of their testimony, for they did not cling to life even in the face of death. Rejoice then, you heavens and those who dwell in them! But woe to the earth and the sea, for the devil has come down to you with great wrath, because he knows that his time is short!"

In both Paul's and John's theology, the rising of the Son also means the descent of the devil. We cannot fully grasp the significance of all of this, but something fundamental that has changed reality has taken place in the heavenlies because of the resurrection of the Son. It is the rising of the Son that has unseated the devil who has come to us. *Luke 10:17-20* says:

> The seventy returned with joy, saying, "Lord, in your name even the demons submit to us!" He said to them, "I watched Satan fall from heaven like a flash of lightning. See, I have given you authority to tread on snakes and scorpions, and over all the power of the enemy; and nothing will hurt you. Nevertheless, do not rejoice at this, that the spirits submit to you, but rejoice that your names are written in heaven."

It is the coming of the Son as the Child that began to confront the power of the devil in a new way, but it is His crucifixion and the resurrection as the Lamb that has unseated Satan and hurled him and his troops to earth. This is a seismic event that is accessible to us only by the revelation of the prophets. But it is enough to say that the Old Testament does not mention exorcisms, and they do not seem to be part of even the ministry of John the Baptist. But when Jesus comes out of the wilderness, the demons begin to flee, as Jesus begins to cast them out. And after the Ascension of Jesus, this power was given to the Church through the anointing of the Holy Spirit, so that any Christian would be able to trample the powers of darkness.

UNDERSTANDING REVELATION

Before the Ascension, the disciples operated through the delegated authority of Jesus, as they had not yet been filled with the Holy Spirit.

The earth protects the woman from the power of the dragon that is chasing the children of Israel. This could mean many things; many Jews did stay within the Roman Empire, but many did flee further. For example, before Muhammed and the rise of Islam, the area of the present-day Saudi Arabia had a powerful Jewish kingdom. But the scattering of the Jews has protected them over the two millennia. There have always been persecutions of the Jews somewhere in the world, but never have they been persecuted everywhere simultaneously.

Enraged, the dragon goes off to make war against the rest of her offspring—those who hold to the testimony of Jesus. These are the Christians. The dragon persecutes Israel, and when it fails to destroy her, it begins to persecute the Church.

We can see how Satan's focus is and has always been to attack God's plan and purposes—whatever they are at any given time. And the devil is always out there to attack the Jews and Christians. Antisemitism and the persecution of Christians have always been satanic efforts to derail the fulfilment of God's promises.

REVELATION 13

Revelation 13 is probably the most famous chapter in the book, as it refers to the beast, the mark of the beast, and the number of the beast —666.

One of my friends, Glenn Metcalf, was an extra in *The Omen* (1976). It is a supernatural horror film that follows Damien, a young child that is the prophesied Antichrist, and when we talk about the number of the beast, we often enter the world of supernatural horror in the minds of the people. Most evangelical Christians associate the number 666 with an end-time Antichrist that has occult powers. Unfortunately, this is based on a serious misinterpretation of Revelation.

Revelation 13 begins with the dragon standing on the shore of the sea. This is continuation from *Revelation 12* and part of the seventh vision. The sea is the sea of nations. John sees a beast with ten horns, seven heads and ten crowns, with each head a blasphemous name on it, rising out of the sea.

The beast has seven heads but ten horns, which means that there are three more horns with crowns than there are heads. Before we come to the significance of this, we must first read Daniel, as this beast resembles a leopard, but it has a bear's feet and a mouth like a lion, with Satan giving the beast a great authority.

In *Daniel 7* the prophet dreams of four beasts. The first beast is like a lion, and it has the wings of an eagle. There is a second beast, which looks like a bear. The third beast is like a leopard, and the fourth beast is the most frightening of them all. It has iron teeth and ten horns.

UNDERSTANDING REVELATION

Most Bible scholars agree that Daniel's four beasts are the Babylonian Empire, the Medo-Persian Empire, the Greek Empire and the fourth, the Roman Empire.

In Daniel's vision, a little horn comes up amongst the horns and uproots three of the first horns. This horn has eyes like the eyes of a man and a mouth that speaks boastfully. But then the Ancient One takes his seat. The horn keeps on boasting, but it is slain.

In Daniel's vision, he sees the Son of Man coming in the clouds of heaven. The Son of Man approaches the Ancient of Days and is led into His presence. He is given authority over all nations, and men in every language worship Him.

Daniel 7:13-14 says:

> As I watched in the night visions, I saw one like a human being coming with the clouds of heaven. And he came to the Ancient One and was presented before him. To him was given dominion and glory and kingship, that all peoples, nations, and languages should serve him. His dominion is an everlasting dominion that shall not pass away, and his kingship is one that shall never be destroyed.

This is Jesus's Ascension after His resurrection. It is when the Child is taken to heaven in Revelation, and also when the Lamb arrives there.

Coming in the clouds can be easily misinterpreted. Yes, He is coming in the clouds, but He is coming to heaven. He is ascending not descending. *Acts 1:9* says about the Ascension of Jesus after the Resurrection:

> When he had said this, as they were watching, he was lifted up, and a cloud took him out of their sight.

This is the cloud that takes the Lamb, the Son, to heaven, to receive the authority after His death and resurrection.

Daniel asks for the true meaning of the vision, as the horn that boasted is waging war against the saints and defeating them. According to the explanation that Daniel receives, the fourth beast is the fourth kingdom that will devour the whole earth. The ten horns are ten kings that will come from it. After that, another king will arise, different

REVELATION 13

from the earlier ones; he will subdue three kings. The saints will be handed over to him for forty-two months.

The symbolism behind the forty-two months is clear: it is the time of the Church's drought, even when it is not a time of judgment. But, eventually, the beast will be destroyed, and the sovereignty, power and greatness under the whole heaven will be handed over to the saints.

Both in *Daniel 7* and in *Revelation 5*, Christ ascends to heaven to take authority, according to Daniel at the time of the reign of the fourth beast. It is certain that this fourth beast is the Roman Empire.

Daniel writes in *verse 8*:

> I was considering the horns, when another horn appeared, a little one coming up among them; to make room for it, three of the earlier horns were plucked up by the roots. There were eyes like human eyes in this horn, and a mouth speaking arrogantly.

Who is the little horn that will replace the three horns? To understand Daniel, we must read him very carefully, and not to insert extra ideas into his vision. For example, we might assume that the little horn will pluck horns number eight, nine and ten in succession to the throne. But that is not in the text; in the vision Daniel might have had no way of knowing the order of the horns anyway, as the beast was simply presented to him as a ten-horned beast with no numbers on the horns.

It is a misinterpretation to interpret this as an alliance between many kings ruling at the same time, as the beast is clearly the Roman Empire. Perhaps many have in recent years committed to this misinterpretation because the EU flag has twelve stars, and the early forms of the EU had fewer members than now. But twelve stars is associated with the Virgin Mary, and it is also a number associated with the apostles and the twelve tribes of Israel.

Based on history, it seems evident that the horns that were plucked were the sixth, seventh and eighth emperors in succession, and the ninth and tenth horns belonged to the same Roman imperial dynasty than the little horn.

God cares deeply about Israel and Jerusalem. That is why He has written so much about them and in such painstaking detail. He also cares about the temples that carried His name in Jerusalem. Much of

UNDERSTANDING REVELATION

the Old Testament prophetic literature warns about the impending destruction of Jerusalem and the First Temple. God was also deeply concerned of the destruction of the Second Temple and the scattering of the Jews across the earth for nearly two millennia.

There is a remarkable year in the history of the Roman Empire, AD 69, when four emperors ruled in succession: Galba, Otho, Vitellius and Vespasian.

The suicide of Emperor Nero in AD 68 was followed by a brief period of civil war, the first Roman civil war since Mark Antony's death in 30 BC. Between June, AD 68 and December, AD 69, Emperors Galba, Otho, and Vitellius rose and fell, the latter overlapping with the accession of Vespasian, who founded the Flavian dynasty in July, AD 69.

Caesar was instrumental in transforming the Roman Republic into the Roman Empire, but it was his son Augustus who became the first Roman Emperor. Caesar was a dictator but not an emperor.

These were the first ten Roman emperors:

1. Augustus (31 BC–AD 14)
2. Tiberius (AD 14–37)
3. Caligula (AD 37–41)
4. Claudius (AD 41–54)
5. Nero (AD 54–68)
6. Galba (AD 68–69)
7. Otho (January–April, AD 69)
8. Aulus Vitellius (July–December, AD 69)
9. Vespasian (AD 69–79)
10. Titus (AD 79–81)

It was during Augustus that Jesus was born, and it was during Augustus that the emperor cult that declared the emperor the son of god began to emerge, putting the new Christian movement on the collision course with the Roman Empire, as apart from Judaism, Christianity was the only religion that did not allow its followers to pay at least lip service to the divinity of the emperor, thereby making Christians enemies of the state. Every other religion within the reach of the Roman Empire had many gods and no major difficulty in adding Roman gods to their

REVELATION 13

pantheon. In fact, the Roman religion often absorbed foreign gods to their pantheon to make submitting to the Roman rule easier.

Hence, we can see how Satan began to tailor the fourth beast to his purposes around the time of Jesus's birth. He was already working on a strategy to stop the plan of God.

Titus destroyed the Second Temple, whilst his father Vespasian went to become the first of the three emperors in the Flavian dynasty. Prior to becoming an emperor, Titus gained renown as a military commander, serving under his father in Judea during the First Jewish–Roman War. The campaign came to a brief halt with the death of Emperor Nero in AD 68, launching Vespasian's bid for the imperial power during the Year of the Four Emperors. When Vespasian was declared emperor on 1 July, AD 69, Titus was left in charge of ending the Jewish rebellion. In AD 70, he besieged and captured Jerusalem, and destroyed the city and the Second Temple. For this achievement Titus was awarded a triumph; the Arch of Titus in Rome commemorates his victory to this day.

But Vespasian was still a general tasked with defeating Judea and Jerusalem when he received a prophecy in Judea that he would become the emperor. Suetonius writes in *The Life of Vespasian*:

> When he consulted the oracle of the god of Carmel in Judaea, the lots were highly encouraging, promising that whatever he planned or wished however great it might be, would come to pass; and one of his high-born prisoners, Josephus by name, as he was being put in chains, declared most confidently that he would soon be released by the same man, who would then, however, be emperor.

Initially, it appears that it was the ninth horn that replaced the sixth, seventh and eighth horns, and it had nothing to do with a little horn. So, was Daniel's prophecy false? But there remains a fascinating detail that to me is one of the greatest testimonies of the amazing accuracy of the Bible prophecy.

Domitian, the younger brother of Titus, who would become the eleventh emperor, was declared emperor in Rome by the celebrating Roman troops after the killing of Vitellius, the eighth emperor (Morgan 2006, 256). This happened before the Senate declared Vespasian, his father, to be the emperor. And when Vespasian was declared emperor in AD 69, he was still in Egypt, and his elder son, Titus, was in Israel, bringing an end to the Jewish rebellion. So Domitian was given a brief time of governing Rome until Vespasian's return (Thompson 1997, 99). So, the little horn Domitian, the eleventh emperor, was declared the emperor before his father Vespasian, who was the ninth horn, and his brother Titus, who was the tenth. The reason why the horn was little is because its initial rise was premature.

In Daniel's vision in *Daniel 7:8*, the horn that uproots the three other horns is Domitian, yet he is not uprooting his father or brother but the three horns that preceded them chronologically in the Year of the Four Emperors. And Vespasian started a new dynasty called the Flavian Dynasty. The Flavian dynasty was unique among the four dynasties of the Principate Era in that it was only one man and his two sons—Vespasian, Titus and Domitian—without any extended or adopted family.

Daniel accurately prophesies that Domitian will be declared the emperor prematurely by calling him the little horn that will grow, as he is the eleventh horn and had to wait for the death of his father and brother before becoming the emperor. How amazingly precise is Daniel's prophecy written down hundreds of years earlier!

Daniel 7:21-25 says:

> As I looked, this horn made war with the holy ones and was prevailing over them, until the Ancient One came; then judgment was given for the holy ones of the Most High, and the time arrived when the holy ones gained possession of the kingdom. This is what he said: "As for the fourth beast, there shall be a fourth kingdom on earth that shall be different from all the other kingdoms; it shall devour the whole earth, and trample it down, and break it to pieces. As for the ten horns, out of this kingdom ten kings shall arise, and another shall arise after them. This one shall be different from the former ones, and shall put down three kings. He shall speak words against the Most High, shall wear out the holy ones of the Most High, and shall attempt to change the sacred seasons and the law; and they shall be given into his power for a time, two times, and half a time."

REVELATION 13

It was during Domitian's reign when the full transition from the dragon trying to destroy the Jews to the dragon making "war on the rest of her children, those who keep the commandments of God and hold the testimony of Jesus", described in *Revelation 12:17*, happened.

It is likely that John completed Revelation during the reign of Domitian, and the prophetic baton concerning world history was transferred from Daniel to John. Although Domitian's was not the first attack against the Church, he marked the beginning of the tribulation when Satan was fully focused on destroying the Early Church. Satan had destroyed Israel and Jerusalem, only to discover that his work had been in vain, as he had been unable to bring complete destruction to the Jews.

Writing before the destruction of the Second Temple, Paul says in *2 Thessalonians 2:1-12* says:

> As to the coming of our Lord Jesus Christ and our being gathered together to him, we beg you, brothers and sisters, not to be quickly shaken in mind or alarmed, either by spirit or by word or by letter, as though from us, to the effect that the day of the Lord is already here. Let no one deceive you in any way; for that day will not come unless the rebellion comes first and the lawless one is revealed, the one destined for destruction. He opposes and exalts himself above every so-called god or object of worship, so that he takes his seat in the temple of God, declaring himself to be God. Do you not remember that I told you these things when I was still with you? And you know what is now restraining him, so that he may be revealed when his time comes. For the mystery of lawlessness is already at work, but only until the one who now restrains it is removed. And then the lawless one will be revealed, whom the Lord Jesus will destroy with the breath of his mouth, annihilating him by the manifestation of his coming. The coming of the lawless one is apparent in the working of Satan, who uses all power, signs, lying wonders, and every kind of wicked deception for those who are perishing, because they refused to love the truth and so be saved. For this reason God sends them a powerful delusion, leading them to believe what is false, so that all who have not believed the truth but took pleasure in unrighteousness will be condemned.

UNDERSTANDING REVELATION

From the early Christian centuries onwards, many have interpreted Paul's words as a prophecy about one end-time Antichrist. But in fact, in a similar vein than Jesus's prophecy in *Matthew 24*, this prophecy has two distinct parts.

Jesus says in *Matthew 24:15-28*:

> So when you see the desolating sacrilege standing in the holy place, as was spoken of by the prophet Daniel (let the reader understand), then those in Judea must flee to the mountains; the one on the housetop must not go down to take what is in the house; the one in the field must not turn back to get a coat. Woe to those who are pregnant and to those who are nursing infants in those days! Pray that your flight may not be in winter or on a sabbath. For at that time there will be great suffering, such as has not been from the beginning of the world until now, no, and never will be. And if those days had not been cut short, no one would be saved; but for the sake of the elect those days will be cut short. Then if anyone says to you, "Look! Here is the Messiah!" or "There he is!"—do not believe it. For false messiahs and false prophets will appear and produce great signs and omens, to lead astray, if possible, even the elect. Take note, I have told you beforehand. So, if they say to you, "Look! He is in the wilderness," do not go out. If they say, "Look! He is in the inner rooms," do not believe it. For as the lightning comes from the east and flashes as far as the west, so will be the coming of the Son of Man. Wherever the corpse is, there the vultures will gather.

The first part of Jesus's prophecy is linked to the destruction of Jerusalem by Titus. The prophecy by Paul, written before the destruction of the Second Temple, also predicts the same event. It was during Vespasian's reign when the Second Temple was destroyed by his son Titus, but the Roman attack began when Vespasian was still a general in the army of Emperor Nero. Effectively, the Second Temple was destroyed as an outcome of Nero's orders even when Nero had already committed suicide when the destruction took place.

If we look at contemporary history, the Brexit process in the UK has taken three Prime Ministers to complete. Each one of them has contributed to the process, from the initial decision by David Cameron

REVELATION 13

to the failure of Theresa May to deliver it, and Boris Johnson actually delivering of it.

In a similar vein, the destruction of the Second Temple was an outcome of many stops and starts, and at least three emperors contributed to the outcome: Nero, Vespasian, and Titus, although Titus was not yet an emperor at the time when he led the effort of destruction. But it was Titus who got the glory for this atrocity, and it is Titus whose arch we can still see in Rome.

It can be difficult to convey historical processes through a vision or prophecy. That is why both the Book of Daniel and Revelation describe them with such detail.

In the second part of His prophecy, Jesus predicts deception in the world and the Church. In a similar vein, Paul predicts deception to come after the destruction of the Second Temple. It is likely that Paul is writing about this to the Thessalonians because he has been reflecting on and praying over the prophecy by Jesus; so similar are the prophecies in structure that Paul should probably not be read here in isolation from Jesus's prophecy.

But in *verses 5-12* of Paul's explanation, there are two things which are rather enigmatic: He who restrains and what or who is being restrained. No conclusive answers to who or what they are exactly have been found. But ultimately, it is God who is restraining the forces of evil.

Verse 8 in Paul's explanation refers to the prophecy about the Branch from Jesse in *Isaiah 11:4* that says:

> But with righteousness he shall judge the poor, and decide with equity for the meek of the earth; he shall strike the earth with the rod of his mouth, and with the breath of his lips he shall kill the wicked.

This verse in Isaiah prophesies that Jesus will judge the unrighteous in the end of times.

In *verses 8* and *9*, calling the "lawless" the "lawless one" is an interpretation by translators, as the Greek text itself simply refers to "the lawless". This is the outcome of most translators assuming that *verses 1-4* and *5-12* are linked together. The verses leave open the possibility that they might be connected, but the connection is not

UNDERSTANDING REVELATION

certain. But we must not automatically assume that "the lawless one" in *verses 1-4* and "the lawless" in *verses 5-12* refer to the same entity. Had that been the case, it would have been rather easy for Paul to make this abundantly clear by carrying the term "the lawless one" to the second part. There must have been a reason for omitting the "one" in the second part of this prophecy. Perhaps Paul was intentionally clear rather than accidentally ambiguous. But Paul is always precise with his language, so we must assume that the omission was probably intentional.

Taken in context, with Paul possibly passing on the prophetic tradition given by Jesus and relating that to the Old Testament prophecies, it seems clear that, in the end of times, Jesus will come to judge the wicked, the deceived and the lawless.

What is problematic for the teaching about one end-time Antichrist is that Paul's writing in *2 Thessalonians* is the only potential reference in the Bible to one end-time Antichrist, and this one reference is rather ambiguous.

Admittedly, *2 Thessalonians 2:1-12* read alone is ambiguous enough to allow an interpretation that there could be one end-time Antichrist. But as so much relies on the correct interpretation of this one Bible passage, we must inspect it more thoroughly.

Is there anywhere else we can look at? As we have seen earlier, John himself seems to refute an idea about one Antichrist in his letters, insisting that there have already been many antichrists that have come from the Church and refused the Lordship of Jesus. And we have already discovered that the beast in Revelation is not the Antichrist but the Roman Empire.

Paul brings clarity to this issue himself. Let Paul explain himself first before we bring along any other interpreters!

Paul writes in *2 Thessalonians 2:5*:

> Do you not remember that I told you these things when I was still with you?

Unfortunately, we do not have access to these unrecorded conversations between Paul and the Thessalonian Christians. Fortunately, we do have access to *1 Thessalonians*, which had been written by AD 52, nearly

REVELATION 13

fifteen years before the First Jewish-Roman War that would bring the destruction of the Second Temple. *2 Thessalonians* was written soon after the first letter, so it is unlikely that Paul's teaching on the matter would have changed much.

Paul writes in *1 Thessalonians 4:13-18*:

> But we do not want you to be uninformed, brothers and sisters, about those who have died, so that you may not grieve as others do who have no hope. For since we believe that Jesus died and rose again, even so, through Jesus, God will bring with him those who have died. For this we declare to you by the word of the Lord, that we who are alive, who are left until the coming of the Lord, will by no means precede those who have died. For the Lord himself, with a cry of command, with the archangel's call and with the sound of God's trumpet, will descend from heaven, and the dead in Christ will rise first. Then we who are alive, who are left, will be caught up in the clouds together with them to meet the Lord in the air; and so we will be with the Lord forever. Therefore encourage one another with these words.

It appears that when Paul wrote *1 Thessalonians*, his expected future time horizon was relatively close, and he seemed to have anticipated Christ's imminent return.

According to church tradition, Paul was martyred before the beginning of the First Jewish-Roman War. So, in time of writing of *1 and 2 Thessalonians*, the destruction of the Second Temple by Titus still lay ahead, and before that, Nero was yet to become the first living emperor to openly declare himself to be god. Until Nero, the emperors had been declared gods only posthumously, much like the Catholic Church will declare someone to be a saint only after their death.

In this relatively short temporal horizon of expectation, it is hard to explain why Paul would not be referring prophetically to the most catastrophic event looming in the horizon, the destruction of the Second Temple, but to something else, and without giving us a clearer explanation. Returning to *2 Thessalonians*, the Greek word *apostasía* has two main meanings, the first being defection, which is translated as "falling away". The other meaning is "rebellion" or "revolt". Translated this way, the rebellion will come first. And after that the lawless will be revealed. This would mean, especially in the light of Jesus's prophecy, that the Jewish Revolt would come first, and after that the lawless would be revealed.

It is possible that Paul is seeing in the Spirit the compound effect of the living emperor declaring himself to be god and the destruction of the Second Temple, and following the twofold structure of Jesus's prophecy, he anticipates an end-time deception, which is, fascinatingly, not that dissimilar to the message of Revelation.

1 Timothy 4:1-5 gives us some clarity on how Paul saw the later times:

> Now the Spirit expressly says that in later times some will renounce the faith by paying attention to deceitful spirits and teachings of demons, through the hypocrisy of liars whose consciences are seared with a hot iron. They forbid marriage and demand abstinence from foods, which God created to be received with thanksgiving by those who believe and know the truth. For everything created by God is good, and nothing is to be rejected, provided it is received with thanksgiving; for it is sanctified by God's word and by prayer.

These *later times* have already taken place. For example, the Catholic Church banned the marriage of priests in the beginning of the second millennium. So, that leaves the time of deception rather open, and we might already be living in the time of deception.

If you read *2 Thessalonians* this way, it does leave the possibility that there might be one end-time Antichrist. But we must remember that Paul does not in fact teach about the coming of the lawless one, but about the coming of the lawless, as adding the "one" is an interpretation by translators and not in the original Greek. And Jesus tells there will be many end-time deceptions and not just one.

As Revelation itself does not teach anything at all about one end-time Antichrist, the teaching about one end-time Antichrist is biblically on a rather shaky footing. Why is this important? I fear that many people will be expecting one end-time Antichrist, and in the absence of his arrival they will miss the actual return of Christ. But we will have a long season of lawlessness before the Second Coming.

REVELATION 13

Returning to Revelation and the beast with ten horns, seven heads and ten crowns, John writes that one of the heads seemed to have a fatal wound, but it had been healed, and the whole world was astonished, and now following the beast. After the death of Nero, in the resulting civil war, it looked for a while that the Roman Empire would fall apart with all these generals fighting in AD 69, but, instead, the empire recovered. In fact, the Jewish rebels drew much encouragement from the suicide of Nero and the resulting Roman civil war.

In *verse 5*, the beast is given authority to speak blasphemies for 42 months after the mortal wound has been healed with the Year of the Four Emperors ending. This links the timing firmly to the destruction of the Second Temple in AD 70, when the symbolic three and a half years of Israel's drought began and would last nearly two millennia. The beast is given power to wage war against the saints and defeat them. To remove all ambiguity, John says in *verse 9*:

> Let anyone who has an ear listen: If you are to be taken captive, into captivity you go; if you kill with the sword, with the sword you must be killed.

This is a clear reference to *Jeremiah 15:1-2*:

> Then the Lord said to me: "Though Moses and Samuel stood before me, yet my heart would not turn toward this people. Send them out of my sight, and let them go! And when they say to you, 'Where shall we go?' you shall say to them: "Thus says the Lord: Those destined for pestilence, to pestilence, and those destined for the sword, to the sword; those destined for famine, to famine, and those destined for captivity, to captivity.""

Jeremiah prophesied the destruction of Jerusalem and says that even the two witnesses, Moses and Samuel—the Law and the Prophets—would be unable to avert the destruction. In *Revelation 13*, the destruction of the Second Temple is replayed from a different perspective.

In *verse 4*, John says that men worshipped the dragon, and they worshipped the beast—by worshipping the gods of Rome people would worship the devil.

UNDERSTANDING REVELATION

Verses 7-8 say,

> Also it was allowed to make war on the saints and to conquer them. It was given authority over every tribe and people and language and nation, and all the inhabitants of the earth will worship it, everyone whose name has not been written from the foundation of the world in the book of life of the Lamb that was slaughtered.

At the time, the Roman Empire ruled much of the inhabited world, and it would continue dominating the world for centuries. Some have difficulties with expressions such as "all the inhabitants of the earth", and conclude that this refers to an end-time new world order, but that misunderstands the biblical language, especially as this is also a reference to Daniel's interpretation of Nebuchadnezzar's dream in *Daniel 2:36-45*:

> This was the dream; now we will tell the king its interpretation. You, O king, the king of kings—to whom the God of heaven has given the kingdom, the power, the might, and the glory, into whose hand he has given human beings, wherever they live, the wild animals of the field, and the birds of the air, and whom he has established as ruler over them all—you are the head of gold. After you shall arise another kingdom inferior to yours, and yet a third kingdom of bronze, which shall rule over the whole earth. And there shall be a fourth kingdom, strong as iron; just as iron crushes and smashes everything, it shall crush and shatter all these. As you saw the feet and toes partly of potter's clay and partly of iron, it shall be a divided kingdom; but some of the strength of iron shall be in it, as you saw the iron mixed with the clay. As the toes of the feet were part iron and part clay, so the kingdom shall be partly strong and partly brittle. As you saw the iron mixed with clay, so will they mix with one another in marriage, but they will not hold together, just as iron does not mix with clay. And in the days of those kings the God of heaven will set up a kingdom that shall never be destroyed, nor shall this kingdom be left to another people. It shall crush all these kingdoms and bring them to an end, and it shall stand forever; just as you saw that a stone was cut from the mountain not by hands, and that it crushed the iron,

REVELATION 13

the bronze, the clay, the silver, and the gold. The great God has informed the king what shall be hereafter. The dream is certain, and its interpretation trustworthy.

Daniel's dream interpretation ends with the crushing of the Roman Empire by the Kingdom of God. But in Daniel's interpretation Nebuchadnezzar rules over all the people in the world, even when we know that, historically, it was not the case. In a similar way, the authority given to the Roman Empire does not need to mean that everything and everyone in the world would have been under the power of the Roman Empire, only that the Roman Empire at the time tended to bring every nation that it encountered under subjugation.

After the destruction of Israel and the Second Temple, as referred to in *Revelation 13:9-10*, the war against the Jews and the saints continued. In AD 115-117, the Jews revolted against the Romans, throughout the empire, including Jerusalem, and in AD 117 Saint Simeon of Jerusalem, the second Bishop of Jerusalem, was crucified there by the proconsul Atticus. In AD 130, Emperor Hadrian visited the ruins of Jerusalem and decided to rebuild it as a city dedicated to Jupiter, the main god of the Romans. Now it would be called Aelia Capitolina. In AD 131, Emperor Hadrian abolished circumcision. In AD 132-135, Simon Bar Kokhba led a revolt against the Romans, controlling the city for three years. He was proclaimed the Messiah. The Romans retook the city, and in AD 136, Hadrian forbid both Jewish and Christian presence in Jerusalem. In AD 136-140, a temple to Jupiter was built on the Temple Mount, and a temple to Venus was built on Calvary, with the holiest places of the Jews and Christians now taken over by the beast.

As *verse 7*, says, the beast was given power against the saints and to conquer them. After this, *verse 10* says:

Here is a call for the endurance and faith of the saints.

This breaks the appearing of the first beast from what will happen next, and because it refers to endurance, it can indicate a lengthy time. After all, it is God asking for patience and not a human being. The war against the saints by the Roman Empire could take some time. It would take hundreds of years.

Then a second beast appears. Unlike the first beast that came out of the sea of nations, this one comes out of the earth. It is qualitatively different from the first one. The sea is the sea of nations. So, a beast coming from the earth must be something else than a nation.

The second beast has two horns of the lamb, but it speaks like the dragon. In *Revelation 5*, the Lamb has seven horns, which are the seven qualities of God—His nature and His perfection. But the second beast has only two horns. The implications are clear. It has only two of these seven qualities.

The second beast looks a little like the Lamb, but it speaks like the Roman Empire. It carries the authority of the Roman Empire, and makes the earth worship the first beast.

Later in *Revelation 16:13, 19:20* and *20:10*, the second beast with two horns of the lamb will be called the false prophet.

Here we encounter some of the most enigmatic verses in the Bible. The second beast performs the miraculous signs of Elijah, which means that it is a false prophet. It orders people to set up an image in honour of the beast. What is the image of the beast that is also made alive? What is the mark of the beast on the right hand or on the forehead? These are the questions Christians have been asking for centuries.

The mark on the forehead clearly refers to slavery. In the Roman Empire, difficult slaves would endure branding. Runaway slaves were even branded or tattooed on their foreheads with the letter *K* ("Stop me, I am fleeing.") or with the letter *F* for *fugitivus*. (Franzen 2013, 357)

Revelation 1:1 says that the letter has been given to God's "servants" via God's "servant" John. But the Greek word for servant, *doulois*, is also translated as slave, and the great dichotomy through Revelation is between the slaves of God and slaves of the beast. So, the mark of the beast is a mark of slavery, but so is the mark of the saints. Only the masters are different. But those who worship the gods of the empire are slaves of Satan.

So, if the beast is an empire, then the horns and crowns represent individual rulers. Following similar lines of interpretation, the second

REVELATION 13

beast is not an individual person, but neither is it a nation. It has two qualities of the Lamb instead of the seven. This implies that the second beast is a corporate entity which can display some of the qualities of the Lamb, but so many others are missing that it does not represent the Lamb.

World history suggests that it has might and knowledge, but it lacks the Spirit of the Lord, wisdom, counsel, understanding, and the fear of the Lord. This is a vastly impoverished Church, which, rather than discipling Christians to submit to Christ, is teaching people to submit to the empire. Later, the impoverished Church will submit to the ways of the Western civilisation that emerged from Rome and become Babylon the Great, the prostitute of *Revelation 17-18* that rides on the beast.

The second beast with two horns, the false prophet, and the great prostitute all refer to the same entity, and in *Revelation 17,* there is a reference to her being the "mother of all whores". I would suggest that the great prostitute and her daughters represent the church system that has fornicated itself by becoming part of the world system of domination to legitimise the earthly use of power. In one sense, we can say that this encompasses large parts of the Western Christendom and even large parts of the Eastern Christendom—wherever the Church has deemed it expedient to submit to the worldly power rather than the Lordship of Jesus.

After all, *Revelation 18:4* says:

> Come out of her, my people, so that you do not take part in her sins, and so that you do not share in her plagues.

It must be possible for God's people to come out of Babylon. This means that many God's people would be part of it, but also that it is possible to leave. This is not an invitation to move to another country, although quite a few British Christians voted to leave the EU because of this verse, perceiving the EU as the beast and believing that a political decision could mark a departure from Babylon.

We must be careful with the words that the second beast is described with, and not take them literally. *Verse 13* says:

UNDERSTANDING REVELATION

> It performs great signs, even making fire come down from heaven to earth in the sight of all.

This is a symbolic book, and this refers to the sign of Elijah. So, this means that the second beast is a prophet. But it is a false prophet, which must mean that unlike Elijah, who slaughtered the prophets of Baal, the false prophet would not truly overcome the Baals of its time.

This foreshadows the idea of the second beast being the false prophet in the end of Revelation.

But what is the image of the beast, and what is the mark of the beast?

John writes in *verse 18*:

> This calls for wisdom: let anyone with understanding calculate the number of the beast, for it is the number of a person. Its number is six hundred sixty-six.

John clarifies that the number of the beast is the number of a person. This means that the number of the beast is linked to a person and helps us identify the beast. The number of the beast refers to one of its horns.

Every Christian generation over the centuries has tried to calculate the number of the beast, often seeking to apply it to prominent people in their time to discover the Antichrist. But according to John, those with wisdom would be able to calculate the number of the beast in John's lifetime. John himself knew the answer. This is not an unsolved puzzle to him. It is a puzzle that John offers himself after seeing the vision. The wise would be able to recognise the beast by this number.

Most Christians know that the number of the beast is 666. But in the early manuscripts, the number of the beast can be either 666 or 616. So, the beast could in fact have two numbers. This indicates that the number itself is not that important, but it aids recognition. Many theories have been made about the three numbers of six standing for the unholy trinity of man, as six is the number one lower than seven, which is the perfect number—the number of God. So, the number six is perceived as the number of man, as he was created on the sixth day.

So, early on, there were two numbers used to identify the beast. And there was some controversy about the number quite early, so around

REVELATION 13

AD 180, Irenaeus, the bishop of Lugdunum, now Lyon in France, who had heard Polycarp, John's disciple, preach, writes in the Book V, Chapter 30 of *Against Heresies* in defence of the number being 666 rather than 616:

> 1. Such, then, being the state of the case, and this number being found in all the most approved and ancient copies [of the Apocalypse], and those men who saw John face to face bearing their testimony [to it]; while reason also leads us to conclude that the number of the name of the beast, [if reckoned] according to the Greek mode of calculation by the [value of] the letters contained in it, will amount to six hundred and sixty and six; that is, the number of tens shall be equal to that of the hundreds, and the number of hundreds equal to that of the units (for that number which [expresses] the digit six being adhered to throughout . . .

The answer to the puzzle is linguistic. Those who have wisdom could speak Hebrew and knew that both numbers 616 and 666 identified Emperor Nero. The Greek version of the name Nero transliterates into Hebrew as נרון קסר, yielding a numerical value of 666. The Latin version of the name Nero transliterates into Hebrew as נרו קסר, yielding 616. So, to know the number of the beast you had to be able to understand Hebrew. You had to know the Book of Daniel to know that he prophesied about Rome as the beast.

But as the Church lost her connection to her Jewish origins, this wisdom was lost, so that two generations later, Irenaeus was puzzled about the alternative number of 616. So, this number is linked to the Roman Empire and not to the second two-horned beast. But why Nero? Why not Titus? Or Vespasian? Or Domitian? I believe that there is a particular reason for the choice of Nero, and it is not only that the number 666 looks like an elegant and symmetric number.

Nero was the first emperor that persecuted Christians. Christians are explicitly mentioned in Suetonius' biography of Emperor Nero as among those punished during Nero's reign. These punishments are generally dated to around AD 64, the year of the Great Fire of Rome. According to church tradition, the apostle Peter was crucified head down in Rome during Nero's persecutions. And Peter was foundational to the Church. Executing Peter on the cross was the most full-frontal attack against Christianity that one could make, apart from the crucifixion of Jesus. And Nero did that. That would surely have stayed in the mind of John. They might have had their arguments in the past, but I am sure John loved Peter dearly.

Until that, Christians had suffered localised persecution, but now persecution had been endorsed by the emperor—one of the beast's horns. And as we will learn, Nero minted a coin that described him as god rather than human being whilst still alive. And that coin would have found its way in the hands of John. And this way the number of the beast will take us to the mark and the image of the beast. It is good to remember that just because the number of the beast is mentioned after the second beast, it does not mean that the number will appear after the second beast has appeared. The number is there merely as a clue to help recognise the first beast.

If we agree that the numbers 666 and 616 refer to Nero, when it comes to the mark and the image of the beast, there are few options to consider. If the beast was the Roman Empire, its power was represented in two ways: through the images of the emperor and through the images of the Greco-Roman gods. These images have been transferred to the Christendom and Western civilisation in two main ways.

First, visually, Christian art is very much a continuation of the art of the Roman Empire, with the images of Christ often resembling the images of Apollo and Mary borrowing visual attributes from the Greco-Roman goddesses, such as Artemis.

The Jews made no images of God at all, and because of her Jewish roots it took at least two hundred years before the Church began to use any kind of images, apart from the rather abstract sign of the fish. *Exodus 20:4-5* commands:

> You shall not make for yourself an idol, whether in the form of anything that is in heaven above, or that is on the earth beneath, or that is in the water under the earth. You shall not bow down to them or worship them.

REVELATION 13

This is the second commandment in the list of the Ten Commandments. Looking at it from this perspective, it seems clear that the second beast would encourage the people to relate to God through an image, making an image into a mediator between man and God.

And for centuries, a multitude of Christians around the world would attempt to relate to God through images, which had been adopted from the Greco-Roman images of gods. Eventually, the Church became nearly entirely an image-based culture, which even restricted the access of Christians to the Bible. There came a point when the Bible was accessible in monasteries only to those monks who were more advanced in their spiritual growth. Jesus might have been Logos, the Word, but the Church became entirely focused on the image.

First, the Church adopted the visual culture of the Roman Empire, and then it adopted its power structures. It became the servant of an earthly empire.

The Reformation brought a break from this visual culture that had become increasingly disconnected from the teachings of the Bible. But although the Reformation disposed of the images, it did not let go of the earthly power structures. Martin Luther, the father of the Reformation, stood on the side of the princes and wrote *Against the Murderous, Thieving Hordes of Peasants*, which endorsed state violence against the peasants. He also wrote *On the Jews and Their Lies* and *Warning against the Jews*. It might have not been Luther's intention, but his antisemitic writings contributed to the acceptance of Nazism in Germany.

This state-endorsing Church that even supported slavery would have been anathema to Jesus. It would have looked like a beast.

All this could be summarised with a coin. For Taylor, the sign of the beast is a coin with an explicit reference to the Roman emperor, and "mark on their right hand" refers to the fact that coins are held in the right hand. In the whole Roman Empire, the only group strongly objecting to the coin with an emperor's image were the Jews. In the first-century Israel, coins with the image of the emperor were rare. Typically, the coins employed vegetal types, such as the lily or the palm tree. Some coins of Herod Philip, Agrippa I, and Agrippa II bear the heads of the Roman emperor or images of themselves, but these coins seem to have been limited to non-Jewish areas. But the Roman-style coinage became the only form of coinage available in Judea in the early to the mid-60s. (Taylor 2009, 580-582) In fact, the Roman-style coinage, and more specifically, the coin of Nero, was one of the causes of the First Jewish-Roman War.

Verses 16 and *17* say:

> Also it causes all, both small and great, both rich and poor, both free and slave, to be marked on the right hand or the forehead, so that no one can buy or sell who does not have the mark, that is, the name of the beast or the number of its name.

Whichever way you may want to interpret this, it is clear is that, one way or other, the mark of the beast refers to the monetary system.

Numismatics are uncertain whether the Roman denarii in fact circulated in Israel before the first Jewish-Roman War. In the east, Romans replaced the local coinage with the Roman coins only when necessary, and the Roman coins would coexist alongside local currency. But by the beginning of the first century, the Roman denarii had already become the exclusive currency in the western Roman Empire. Romans began to print them in large quantities only after the destruction of the Second Temple. Before that, the denarius coin itself was rare, although the denomination was well known. In Asia Minor, the principal coins were cistophorus, and to much lesser extent, the Roman denarius. Cistophorus employed imperial iconography, usually with the head of the Roman emperor on its obverse. With few exceptions, such as the city of Laodicea, the bronze coinage in Asia Minor also employed imperial imagery. In eastern Anatolia, most of the silver coinage was minted in Caesaria, Cappadocia, and bore from the reign of Tiberius (AD 14–37) the head of the Roman emperor. (Taylor 2009, 583-586)

Before the destruction of the Second Temple, it was entirely possible to avoid using the Roman money in Judea, and a coin with Caesar's image that the Pharisees and Herodians showed to Jesus in Mark 12 would probably have been quite rare.

The silver coinage in Roman Syria came from Antioch and Tyre. The Tyrian shekel had the highest silver content, which was consistently over 95%. The Antiochene silver displayed the imperial

REVELATION 13

portrait from the time of Augustus. The Tyrian shekel featured the bust of Melqart (the Phoenician Hercules) with standing eagle on the reverse. Judea was the only place, aside from Nabatea, where ordinary people could avoid the use of Roman or Roman-style coinage. Eventually, some Jews became uncomfortable even with the image of Melqart. After the First Jewish-Roman War began, the rebels began melting these coins and defacing them. (ibid., 587-588, 591)

Around AD 60, the quantity of silver coins produced by the Tyre mint collapsed, and the ones produced were mainly designated for the Second Temple. The Tyre shekel was replaced with the Antioch tetradrachm as part of Nero's monetary initiatives. The Antioch tetradrachm featured the portrait, regnal year, and the name of Nero. And to make things worse, the coins depicted him as divine rather than human being. Until now, the Jews in Judea had been able to avoid the direct use of Roman money. Now, they were forced to use coins that depicted the emperor as a divine being. Within a decade, silver money in the region silver joined the rest of the empire, and it became impossible to buy and sell without the image of the beast (ibid., 591, 592, 593)

So, Nero's coin helped to trigger the Jewish-Roman War, leading to the destruction of Jerusalem, the Second Temple, the death of a million Jews and the enslavement of tens of thousands of them. One group of God's people, many of the Jews, had decided to stand up against the beast because they refused to worship the image of the beast through using Nero's coin. Now they had been wiped out by the beast. For every Jew, Rome would have looked like a demonic monster after that.

There is the issue of the apostle John disappearing from the story of the Early Church; he features in the beginning of the Book of Acts but then vanishes. Yet, according to church tradition, he appeared in Ephesus after the martyrdom of Paul. What happened to John before that? Why was he not leading the church in Jerusalem alongside Peter and James, the brother of Jesus? Was he not the disciple that Jesus loved?

John 19:25-27 gives us an answer:

UNDERSTANDING REVELATION

> Meanwhile, standing near the cross of Jesus were his mother, and his mother's sister, Mary the wife of Clopas, and Mary Magdalene. When Jesus saw his mother and the disciple whom he loved standing beside her, he said to his mother, "Woman, here is your son." Then he said to the disciple, "Here is your mother." And from that hour the disciple took her into his own home.

It seems that John might have stayed in Judea perhaps until the death of Mary or until the beginning of the First Jewish-Roman War. Hence, John would have been a relative newcomer to the Greco-Roman world, possibly traveling to Asia Minor only just before AD 70. Until that time, he would have been surrounded by the Jews who abhorred using the Roman money.

Imagine John holding the coin that called Nero god in his hand for the first time. Would he have even touched it?

All the evidence points to the image of the beast being the image on the coin of an emperor declared to be god.

But what is the mark of the beast on the right hand or the forehead? The rules of interpretation that Revelation gives to us dictate it not to be a visible mark; those who participate in the Roman idolatry were marked for destruction by God.

As I have mentioned, the opening lines of Revelation say that the contents of the book were disclosed to John, who is called a "slave" of God. Christian readers were also called God's slaves—although many Bibles translate the Greek word *doulois* as "servant", it was the ordinary term for someone who was a slave rather than a free person. God's slaves received His name on their foreheads (Koester 2008, 768-769)

Revelation 7:2-3 says:

> I saw another angel ascending from the rising of the sun, having the seal of the living God, and he called with a loud voice to the four angels who had been given power to damage earth and sea, saying, "Do not damage the earth or the sea or the trees, until we have marked the servants of our God with a seal on their foreheads."

REVELATION 13

The mark on the servants of God is not a physical mark. Why would we expect the mark of the beast to be a physical mark? This is contradictory to the principles of interpretation John has presented to us.

Nero ruled only briefly, but the beast would persecute Christians for centuries, and until Constantine, the first Christian emperor, the monetary system of the Roman Empire was directly linked to the Roman idolatry that claimed the emperor to be the son of god. For hundreds of years, Christians could buy and sell only by using money that promoted the idea that an emperor was god and Rome itself was divine.

There is one valid objection to this interpretation, and it is that we will encounter the beast and those who worshipped his image in *Revelation 19*—in the end of times. How could Nero's coin be used in the end times?

The first thing to note is that in Revelation 19 the second beast is called the false prophet. The change of title signifies development. Also, the first beast is depicted as a shape-shifting monster. Whereas the empires Daniel saw in his vision were clearly defined, the beast in Revelation has bits of the earlier empires. This means that unlike the earlier empires, it does not have a clearly defined shape. It keeps on changing and shifting.

Put simply, over the centuries, the Roman Empire has grown to become the Western civilisation. And in that process, it was the false prophet that helped make the financial markets alive.

Rome was sacked in AD 410. This can give us the impression that AD 410 meant the destruction of the Roman Empire. But that is not the case. The Visigoths could sack Rome only because it had shrunk to a small town of 50,000 residents. The capital of the empire had been moved to Constantinople, which is the modern-day Istanbul. And the eastern branch of the empire continued uninterrupted as the Byzantine Empire for another thousand years. This empire was centred on Asia Minor, the new centre of Christianity, and it would withstand Islam for centuries. And the lost European parts of the empire were not lost to Christianity; in fact, even the Visigoths who sacked Rome had already converted to Christianity at the time of sacking, only they followed Arian rather than Catholic theology.

UNDERSTANDING REVELATION

And even after Constantine, the coins would have looked quite similar than the earlier pagan coins.

If we accept that the image of the beast is linked to the monetary system, how could the image of the beast become alive? And what possible role could the two-horned beast have in making it alive?

Now we are coming to one of the most fascinating chapters in the world's financial history. The origins of modern banking can be traced to medieval and early Renaissance Italy, to the rich cities in the north, like Florence, Lucca, Siena, Venice, and Genoa. The Bardi and Peruzzi families dominated banking in the fourteenth century Florence, establishing branches in many other parts of Europe. One of the most famous Italian banks was the Medici Bank, set up by Giovanni di Bicci de' Medici in 1397. The earliest known state deposit bank, Banco di San Giorgio (Bank of St. George), was founded in 1407 at Genoa, Italy.

The birth of the modern banking system was intimately linked to the Church, which was the first main customer of banking services. The Church needed international banking services to transfer money given to the Church to Italy safely. This helped to build an international banking network, which was initially controlled by the Italian banks. The cardinals and many churchmen also needed it to hide their wealth, as they were not really supposed to own any property, and any new pope could easily confiscate their properties. So, these churchmen became the customers of international banks that could hide the money much more effortlessly than a churchman could conceal a property. Also, much of the medieval and early Renaissance art in Italian churches, and often the churches themselves, were created with the money the rich men paid to secure a shorter stay in the purgatory, so in a very real way, the Church ended up selling salvation. (Parks 2013, 20-59)

Without the Church in Rome, the modern banking system could look quite different from what it is today, especially as many of the banking arrangements were generated to circumvent the ban on interest. Even the modern currency exchange system was developed partially to avoid the ban by Church on usury.

Our current, global financial system was created with the vital and decisive contribution by the Church in Rome. Today, it is fully electronic, and it is increasingly utilising artificial intelligence.

REVELATION 13

So, Nero's coin has survived nearly two thousand years, and it has become alive through financial markets that are able to destroy whole economies in one day. We might have lost the emperor, but the world worships the image itself. Jesus says in *Matthew 6:24*:

> No one can serve two masters; for a slave will either hate the one and love the other, or be devoted to the one and despise the other. You cannot serve God and wealth.

These two masters are in direct competition with each other. If you serve money, you worship the image of the beast, because the worship of money still releases the same destructive and oppressive forces than thousands of years ago. It keeps the world in slavery.

Paul says in *1 Timothy 6:10*:

> For the love of money is a root of all kinds of evil, and in their eagerness to be rich some have wandered away from the faith and pierced themselves with many pains.

One of the most disheartening things about today's world is that nearly everything we buy is somehow connected to slavery and oppression.

Every imperial system has elements of the beast. First, the Roman imperial systems was Christianised, then it continued with the Holy Roman Empire and the Byzantium, the different colonial empires and every empire that preaches Christ but practises exploitation through domination. In one sense, the whole Christendom as an imperial system has functioned as the beast, as it has trampled down other nations and continents, even taking lives of hundreds of millions of people through wars and exploitation. *Exodus 20:7* says:

> You shall not make wrongful use of the name of the Lord your God, for the Lord will not acquit anyone who misuses his name.

The imperial Christendom as a whole, which has for hundreds of years been the dominant power in the world and operated through the logic of exploitation of nations, is still carrying the name of Christ, thereby making a wrongful use of His name, and breaking the Ten Commandments every day.

UNDERSTANDING REVELATION

And we think that God does not care, even when it was for similar reasons that God brought destruction to Israel, Judea, and Jerusalem. We often assume that they were destroyed by their idolatry, but linked to the prophets' message against idolatry was always a message against oppression and exploitation of the poor.

According to *Matthew 25:31-46*, the judgment of the nations is based on their relationship to oppression:

> When the Son of Man comes in his glory, and all the angels with him, then he will sit on the throne of his glory. All the nations will be gathered before him, and he will separate people one from another as a shepherd separates the sheep from the goats, and he will put the sheep at his right hand and the goats at the left. Then the king will say to those at his right hand, "Come, you that are blessed by my Father, inherit the kingdom prepared for you from the foundation of the world; for I was hungry and you gave me food, I was thirsty and you gave me something to drink, I was a stranger and you welcomed me, I was naked and you gave me clothing, I was sick and you took care of me, I was in prison and you visited me." Then the righteous will answer him, "Lord, when was it that we saw you hungry and gave you food, or thirsty and gave you something to drink? And when was it that we saw you a stranger and welcomed you, or naked and gave you clothing? And when was it that we saw you sick or in prison and visited you?" And the king will answer them, "Truly I tell you, just as you did it to one of the least of these who are members of my family, you did it to me." Then he will say to those at his left hand, "You that are accursed, depart from me into the eternal fire prepared for the devil and his angels; for I was hungry and you gave me no food, I was thirsty and you gave me nothing to drink, I was a stranger and you did not welcome me, naked and you did not give me clothing, sick and in prison and you did not visit me." Then they also will answer, "Lord, when was it that we saw you hungry or thirsty or a stranger or naked or sick or in prison, and did not take care of you?" Then he will answer them, "Truly I tell you, just as you did not do it to one of the least of these, you did not do it to me." And these will go away into eternal punishment, but the righteous into eternal life.

REVELATION 13

In Britain, in 2006, shortly before the bicentenary of the 1807 Abolition Act, Archbishop Williams apologised for the Church's role in the transatlantic slave trade. Many bishops and other clerics had substantial plantation and slave holdings in the Caribbean, making them perhaps one of the largest institutional bodies involved. Some clerics were compensated for their loss of slaves in the 1834 act to the extent that they were able to personally fund the building of new churches in England. And it was not just the Anglican Church but many other churches that were involved in slave trade.

What kind of church endorses slavery? A church that behaves like a false prophet, a prostitute Church. For hundreds of years the Church in England, the Catholic Church, and many other churches started in Europe brought the name of God to disrepute with their leaders practising the very opposite of what Jesus taught. Jesus came to set the prisoners free, but the Church instead chose to support enslaving people who were free, put them in chains, forcibly remove them from their homeland and eradicate their identity so much so that millions of African Americans are unaware of their roots even today.

The beast of the ancient Roman Empire was Christianised, but it is still dominating; it is only now that the West has become fearful of other civilisations.

What John is talking about is the Church that is so intertwined with the empire that it is difficult to see the difference between their goals and objectives.

There is another illuminating perspective on the image of the beast. The encounter with the image of the beast thoroughly transformed the Church. When Christianity left the confines of Judea, it also would eventually leave a religion and culture that was focused on the Word and prohibited making any images of God. Because of that, the Orthodox Judaism still bans the creation of certain types of graven images of people, angels, or astronomical bodies, whether they are used as idols or not.

Islam has followed this path sometimes to extremity, and that is one of the reasons Islamic art is known for beautiful geometric patterns, as it often sought to create beauty without creating potential idols.

A Roman funeral graffiti, written around AD 260, says, "*Paule ed Petre petite pro victore*"—"Paul and Peter, pray for Victor", invoking the two apostles for salvation. Already, in the middle of the third century, some Christians believed that that the martyred apostles can intercede in heaven for the believers, and that they can be spiritually present with the living on earth at the same time, with this spiritual presence being objectified in the objects of matter. The uniqueness of Christ's death and resurrection was jeopardised. (Peter Lampe 2015, 285, 288-289)

The transition from word culture to image culture brought new forms of worship and concepts that were contradictory to the Bible. The Christianisation of the pagan image took place everywhere. The first church Jesus addressed in Revelation was Ephesus, where the Mary was merged with Artemis. Even Apollo became Christ. And over the centuries, hundreds of millions of Christians have perceived a physical image of Christ or Mary to be the connecting point between man and God—when the Bible is clearly teaching that we as human beings ourselves are the images of God.

Genesis 1:27 says:

> So God created humankind in his image, in the image of God
> he created them; male and female he created them.

The positive reason for this commandment is that we are already images of God, with us being male and female and brought through marriage to unity, bringing a wonderful understanding of the Trinity. God does not need dead images; only the living and breathing ones will do.

I don't think God has an issue with images as such. But through centuries they have often been seen as the mediators between man and God, especially when there has been lack in preaching the Word.

Once the Roman Empire was Christianised, the image of Mary and the image of Christ became the images of an earthly empire and often tools for oppression. And when Christianity becomes a medium for oppression, even the image of Christ can become the image of an antichrist.

Theodosian Code compiled the Roman laws under the Christian emperors. It came to force in AD 439. It says in XVI 1.2.:

REVELATION 13

> It is Our will that all the peoples who are ruled by the administration of Our Clemency shall practice that religion which the divine Peter the Apostle transmitted to the Romans ... The rest, whom We adjudge demented and insane, shall sustain the infamy of heretical dogmas, their meeting places shall not receive the name of churches, and they shall be smitten first by divine vengeance and secondly by the retribution of Our own initiative.

What is striking is that Revelation begins the story of the Church in Ephesus, and then continues it with the false prophet leading the Church astray to embrace the Roman Empire, part of which also took place in Ephesus.

When Nestorius arrived in Constantinople, the imperial capital, from Antioch, he was astonished by the excessive worship and near-deification of Mary, bolstered by the imperial support. The Council of Ephesus's Christological statements that we referred to earlier were largely theological adjustments necessary to accommodate the Virgin's veneration. Cultic devotion to the Virgin was part of the religious landscape of the eastern Mediterranean at least fifty years before the Council of Ephesus. Gregory of Nyssa records the earliest known Marian apparition before AD 380. According to the fifth-century church historian Sozomen, the healing power, miracles, dreams, and visions were accredited to Mary, the Mother of God in Constantinople. (Shoemaker 2008, 71-73)

Sozomen, a church historian born in AD 400, writes in *Ecclesiastical History*, Book 7 Chapter 5:

> Soon after the enactment of this law, Theodosius went to Constantinople. The Arians, under the guidance of Demophilus, still retained possession of the churches. Gregory of Nazianzen presided over those who maintain the "consubstantiality" of the Holy Trinity, and assembled them together in a little dwelling, which had been altered into the form of a house of prayer, by those who held the same opinions and had a like form of worship. It subsequently became one of the most conspicuous in the city, and is so now, not only for the beauty and number of its structures, but also for the advantages accruing to it from the visible manifestations of God. For the power of God was

there manifested, and was helpful both in waking visions and in dreams, often for the relief of many diseases and for those afflicted by some sudden transmutation in their affairs. The power was accredited to Mary, the Mother of God, the holy virgin, for she does manifest herself in this way. The name of Anastasia was given to this church, because, as I believe, the Nicene doctrines which were fallen into disuse in Constantinople, and, so to speak, buried by reason of the power of the heterodox, arose from the dead and were again quickened through the discourses of Gregory; or, as I have heard, some affirm with assurance that one day, when the people were met together for worship in this edifice, a pregnant woman fell from the highest gallery, and was found dead on the spot; but that, at the prayer of the whole congregation, she was restored to life, and she and the infant were saved. On account of the occurrence of this divine marvel, the place, as some assert, obtained its name.

When Artemis became Mary, she also received divine attributes. On human level, there had been a good reason for this transition—Christians were not persecuted because they worshipped Jesus. They were persecuted because they worshipped *only* Jesus. Hence Mary became the bridge between Christianity and the Roman religion through Artemis, making Christians more acceptable. After the Christianisation of the Roman Empire, this logic began to work in the diverse direction: it was possible to worship Artemis if you called her Mary.

The Roman Church itself began to take the shape of the empire. By the first century the Roman Church had grown into several discrete communities. It was as late as AD 235 that we encounter the commemoration of the first monarchic bishop of Rome. But papal monarchy was still contested in AD 251, and by the end of the third century, there were still at least twenty distinct Christian communities in Rome. The first Christian Emperor Constantine began to shape the church landscape, and he gifted the great basilica of St. John to the Bishop of Rome as part of Romanizing the Church. The single great beneficiary of Constantine's generosity was the bishop who became a city magnate. A century before Constantine, the Roman Church had possessed no central authority figure. Alliance with Constantine

REVELATION 13

cemented the Roman bishop's personal position and enhanced the power of his office. This is Constantine's enduring contribution to the development of the papacy. (Leadbetter 2002, 3, 5, 11, 12, 14)

Christianity began to adopt all Roman imperial patterns. From Emperor Constantine on, the Church embraced the imperial structures so completely that until the early twentieth century the Church still gathered in buildings modelled according to Roman court houses. Consequently, we have built very different church communities than Jesus and the foundational apostles prescribed.

Also, the Church began to convert pagan temples to cathedrals. The Great Mosque of Damascus was first the location of an Aramaean temple dedicated to the god Hadad, which was dedicated to Zeus after the successful military campaign of Alexander the Great. In AD 391, it was converted to the Cathedral of Saint John. (Sobczak 2015, 311) One of the best known and preserved conversions is the Pantheon in Rome.

So, the Church adopted the monarchic hierarchies and converted the temples of the Roman Empire. It began to reflect the empire in everything that it did. The persecuted, underground movement had now become the persecutor and part of the empire.

When we are images of Christ, we reflect Christ. When we are images of the empire, we reflect the empire.

In *Revelation 17*, we will see the consequences of this adultery between the beast and the Church through the prostitute that is riding on the beast.

On one level, Revelation tracks the development of the seven churches through time and divides the Church from beginning to end between the faithful and the unfaithful. One of the big mistakes in the interpretation of Revelation is seeking to fit it all in one end-time generation, as in many ways, Revelation captures the great developments in the world, Church, and salvation history.

It is good to remember that God is only concerned of our worship of the image and not of the images themselves. But it is the Word that restrains the images, so that they remain as images. The idolatry of the medieval Church was not the images but not having the Bible.

Paul writes in *Colossians 3:5*:

UNDERSTANDING REVELATION

> Put to death, therefore, whatever in you is earthly: fornication, impurity, passion, evil desire, and greed (which is idolatry).

Perhaps Satan's deception with money works so well because we all need it as a medium of exchange. Often, it can look like God's blessing. And sometimes, it really is.

In my experience, the wealthy churches and their leaders grow accustomed to achieving good things through money. I have met many church leaders whose faith has withered after their church has been blessed with great wealth. Before, these leaders achieved things through prayer and fasting, now they are achieving things through mammon. But as Jesus says, we cannot serve both God and mammon.

The Eighth Vision

REVELATION 14

Revelation 14 describes the expansion of the Church on earth. It begins with a vision of the 144,000 Jews on Mount Zion. They stand there with the Lamb, and the Lamb's name and the Father's name are written on their foreheads.

No one else could learn their new song. The number 144,000 indicates the fullness of the salvation for the Jews. These are the Jews who have kept themselves pure from idolatry—hence there is no Dan who introduced idolatry to Israel in the list of *Revelation 7*. They are described as the first fruits.

If they are the first fruits, then *these* 144,000 must be the Jews who first came to Christ as the first fruit of Jesus's mission. The gospel was preached first to the Jews, and not all Jews rejected it. The first church was a Jewish church.

Then John sees another angel flying mid-air, and he has the eternal gospel to proclaim to those who live on the earth—to every nation, tribe, language, and people. This angel presents the time after the first fruits, the spreading of the gospel to the Gentiles.

This is a new vision. It begins a new story. It is not a chronological continuation of what happened in *Revelation 13*. Instead, it begins from the beginning of the giving of the gospel to the Jews and accounts the preaching of it to every nation. But then it speeds to the end-times. This is because the inevitable outcome of the preaching of the gospel is not just salvation but also judgment.

Verse 8 says:

UNDERSTANDING REVELATION

Fallen! Fallen is Babylon the Great, which made all the nations drink the maddening wine of her adulteries.

Verses 9-13 continue:

> A third angel followed them and said in a loud voice: "If anyone worships the beast and its image and receives its mark on their forehead or on their hand, they, too, will drink the wine of God's fury, which has been poured full strength into the cup of his wrath. They will be tormented with burning sulfur in the presence of the holy angels and of the Lamb. And the smoke of their torment will rise for ever and ever. There will be no rest day or night for those who worship the beast and its image, or for anyone who receives the mark of its name." This calls for patient endurance on the part of the people of God who keep his commands and remain faithful to Jesus. Then I heard a voice from heaven say, "Write this: Blessed are the dead who die in the Lord from now on."

In the New Testament, Babylon refers to Rome, and Sodom and Gomorrah refer to Jerusalem. Peter writes in *1 Peter 5:13*:

> Your sister church in Babylon, chosen together with you, sends you greetings; and so does my son Mark.

Peter is not writing from the ancient Babylon in the present-day Iraq. Instead, he is writing from Rome. Augustine of Hippo wrote *The City of God* in the early fifth century. He writes in Chapter 18:

> Perhaps our readers expect us to say something about this so great delusion wrought by the *demons*; and what shall we say but that men must fly out of the midst of *Babylon*? *Isaiah 48:20* For this prophetic precept is to be understood spiritually in this sense, that by going forward in the living *God*, by the steps of *faith*, which works by *love*, we must flee out of the city of this world, which is altogether a society of ungodly *angels* and men. Yea, the greater we see the power of the *demons* to be in these depths, so much the more tenaciously must we cleave to the Mediator through whom we ascend from these lowest to the highest places.

REVELATION 14

At this point the Roman Empire had already been Christianised; yet Augustine saw the work of demons around himself and wrote about escaping Babylon.

He continues in Chapter 22:

> To be brief, the city of *Rome* was founded, like another *Babylon*, and as it were the daughter of the former *Babylon*, by which *God* was pleased to conquer the whole world, and subdue it far and wide by bringing it into one fellowship of government and *laws*.

On surface, Revelation seems to refer to the future falling of Babylon as the city of Rome. But this reference has a twofold purpose. At this point, Revelation reminds that participating in the Roman idolatry has eternal consequences. The patience of the saints means that it will take time before Babylon's fall and the persecution will end. Initially, Babylon will fall because of the Christian takeover of the Roman Empire. But we will see later that although Babylon has fallen, the story of Babylon has not ended, but it will continue with the story of Christendom. Much like when Christians took over Ephesus and Artemis became Mary, when Christians took over Rome, the Church was Romanized, and it became Babylon. But this will happen later.

What will perplex John later is that Babylon will fall again in *Revelation 18*.

We can see the meaning of Sodom, Gomorrah and Babylon clearly when we contrast them with New Jerusalem. We will see how Sodom, Gomorrah and Babylon represent failed spiritual systems and corruption of God's plan for Israel and the Church.

The third angel warns that if anyone worships the beast, his image, or receives his mark on the forehead, he too will drink of the wine of God's fury.

What is interesting is that the second beast with two horns is not mentioned in the fall of Babylon at this point. Neither is the false prophet mentioned. But the image of the beast is already there. So, Babylon will fall first time when the beast with the two horns—the false prophet—has not yet fully emerged.

UNDERSTANDING REVELATION

So, this vision indicates that many of those who do not compromise with the beast, will suffer martyrdom. But before that, it gives the encouraging message that Babylon will fall.

Isaiah 21:9 says:

> "Look, there they come, riders, horsemen in pairs!" Then he responded, "Fallen, fallen is Babylon; and all the images of her gods lie shattered on the ground."

Jeremiah 51:6-8 exhorts:

> Flee from the midst of Babylon, save your lives, each of you! Do not perish because of her guilt, for this is the time of the Lord's vengeance; he is repaying her what is due. Babylon was a golden cup in the Lord's hand, making all the earth drunken; the nations drank of her wine, and so the nations went mad. Suddenly Babylon has fallen and is shattered; wail for her! Bring balm for her wound; perhaps she may be healed.

With Isaiah we can see the nature of Babylon's fall. All the carved images of her gods will be broken to the ground. By referring to these prophecies, John is prophesying that through the patience of the saints the Roman system of idolatry will be broken.

When we read Revelation, we must be careful with it, as every shift in perspective matters, and it might indicate a different time. If there is one thing much of interpretation has missed, it is temporal developments, and this results in grave misinterpretations. This reminds me of the flaws in social sciences, which often seek to present reality through static models and are not always that good in capturing temporal change.

In the previous vision John sees the Church seduced by the empire, in this vision he sees the Church overcoming the empire.

The fact that the visions have been explained in one order does not mean necessarily that this would somehow signify a chronological order of their fulfilment. The words "Then I looked" in the beginning of *Revelation 14* mean only that John saw what he saw in *Revelation 14* after what he saw in *Revelation 12* and *13*. It is common for prophets to see visions in a non-chronological order when it comes to fulfilment.

REVELATION 14

In my personal life, the prophecies I have received have often been fulfilled in reverse order. I account for this in my book *Five Movements: Winning Your Battle for Your Prophetic Gift*. This non-chronological order of fulfilment is often the hardest and the most painful lesson to learn about the gift of prophecy.

There could be many years on both sides of the word "Then", as the biblical narrative can often compress time to focus on the main narrative points.

Personally, I have received parts of the same prophecy in different times over a thirty-year period. Yet, if I were to tell the story of these prophecies, I would automatically skip over the lengthy intervals when the Holy Spirit has not spoken to me about this one issue to bring the prophetic narrative together. And each time the Holy Spirit has spoken to me about this issue over the years, He has illuminated it from a new perspective.

It seems clear that Revelation accounts the story of both the faithful and the unfaithful Church. That is why there are seven churches in the beginning of the story. Even in the beginning of the story of the Church, the different parts of the Church will struggle with corruption and near-apostasy.

Like the unfaithful Judah and Israel, the unfaithful Church does not cease to be called by His Name.

But whereas the previous chapter concentrates on the deception brought by the second beast with two horns, this chapter concentrates on the fate of the faithful in contrast to the fate of the unfaithful.

John says that this calls for the patient endurance on the part of the saints to remain faithful to Jesus.

Verses 14-16 say:

> Then I looked, and there was a white cloud, and seated on the cloud was one like the Son of Man, with a golden crown on his head, and a sharp sickle in his hand! Another angel came out of the temple, calling with a loud voice to the one who sat on the cloud, "Use your sickle and reap, for the hour to reap has come, because the harvest of the earth is fully ripe." So the one who sat on the cloud swung his sickle over the earth, and the earth was reaped.

UNDERSTANDING REVELATION

After the first fall of Rome as Babylon, the harvest is ripe, and looking back in history, we have lived in the era of spreading the gospel since the fall of the Roman paganism.

The Christian takeover led to the partial corruption of the Church, but it also enabled the preaching of the gospel in all parts of the world. Even now, the earth is still being harvested. But at the same time, the harvest of God's wrath is being gathered. There are two harvests taking place in the world, one for salvation and one for damnation.

The first harvest of salvation is gathered first by one angel in *verses 15-16*. Only after that, starting in *verse 17*, the harvest for damnation is gathered by another angel, fulfilling the prophecies in *Joel 3* and *Isaiah 63*.

Joel 3:12-13 prophesies:

> Let the nations rouse themselves, and come up to the valley of Jehoshaphat; for there I will sit to judge all the neighboring nations. Put in the sickle, for the harvest is ripe. Go in, tread, for the wine press is full. The vats overflow, for their wickedness is great.

Isaiah 63:3 says:

> I have trodden the wine press alone, and from the peoples no one was with me; I trod them in my anger and trampled them in my wrath; their juice spattered on my garments, and stained all my robes.

This is a vision from the beginning of the harvest in Judea through the world evangelism to the final judgment. It tells the story of salvation, starting from Judea, expanding to the nations, overcoming Rome, and the subsequent advancement of the gospel and the delayed judgment of earth.

Luke 24:45-47 says:

> Then he opened their minds to understand the scriptures, and he said to them, "Thus it is written, that the Messiah is to suffer and to rise from the dead on the third day, and that repentance

REVELATION 14

and forgiveness of sins is to be proclaimed in his name to all nations, beginning from Jerusalem."

Matthew 24:14 says:

> And this good news of the kingdom will be proclaimed throughout the world, as a testimony to all the nations; and then the end will come.

Whilst the prostitute Church has concentrated on accumulating wealth and power in spiritual adultery with the earth's kings, the true Church has and will focus on the eternal destiny of people in all the nations, participating in the reaping of the harvest.

It is because of this harvest of salvation that the harvest of wrath will be delayed.

I sometimes wonder if the number of the saved will have to at least equal the number of the fallen angels, but as God's love is abundant, it might exceed that.

Verse 14 says that it is the Son of Man Himself who has the sickle in His hand—it is the Lord Jesus Himself, who will lead this harvesting, and this harvesting will be His focus on earth. The Church must remember this especially at this time when our focus has shifted —in good and bad—to what is taking place on earth in our lifetime. One group of Christians is focused on seeking earthly justice for the oppressed, another group of Christians is focused on accumulating wealth. But Christ is primarily focused on gathering an eternal harvest.

The central focus of the Church has always been to preach the gospel to the nations to help bring in the harvest of salvation. Obviously, this includes living in such a manner that is not contradictory to the gospel and loving our neighbours. Being heaven-focused does not mean being loveless on earth.

The Ninth Vision

REVELATION 15

We have taken a long break from the end-time plagues, but *Revelation 15* returns to them. It begins the time of the final judgments.

Hebrews 1:2 says, "But in these last days he has spoken to us by a Son". This means that the last days began with the crucifixion and resurrection of the Son. We must remember that we have been living in the last days since the first century.

Soon, seven angels will bring seven final plagues, and with this the wrath of God will have ended.

The saints are singing the Song of Moses and the Song of the Lamb. They have been victorious over the beast, over his image and over his name. Initially, this group seems fully identified with the martyrs and those who have prevailed over the Roman Empire. But it is a similar group than the 144,000. Like the 144,000 of Israel, that represent the saved of Israel, those who have overcome the beast represent the victorious Church.

The juxtaposing of these two groups—the saved Jews and the saved Gentiles—goes through Revelation.

The Song of Moses can be found in *Deuteronomy 32:1-43*, and it was composed just before Moses' death. It is a song of those who are about to enter their Promised Land. But unlike the Promised Land of Israel, this is the song of those who are about to enter the Final and Eternal Promised Land.

Verses 5-6 say:

> Yet his degenerate children have dealt falsely with him, a perverse and crooked generation. Do you thus repay the Lord,

UNDERSTANDING REVELATION

O foolish and senseless people? Is not he your father, who created you, who made you and established you?

Verses 15-22 say:

> Jacob ate his fill; Jeshurun grew fat, and kicked. You grew fat, bloated, and gorged! He abandoned God who made him, and scoffed at the Rock of his salvation. They made him jealous with strange gods, with abhorrent things they provoked him. They sacrificed to demons, not God, to deities they had never known, to new ones recently arrived, whom your ancestors had not feared. You were unmindful of the Rock that bore you; you forgot the God who gave you birth. The Lord saw it, and was jealous; he spurned his sons and daughters. He said: "I will hide my face from them, I will see what their end will be; for they are a perverse generation, children in whom there is no faithfulness. They made me jealous with what is no god, provoked me with their idols. So I will make them jealous with what is no people, provoke them with a foolish nation. For a fire is kindled by my anger, and burns to the depths of Sheol; it devours the earth and its increase, and sets on fire the foundations of the mountains."

Verse 43 says:

> Praise, O heavens, his people, worship him, all you gods! For he will avenge the blood of his children, and take vengeance on his adversaries; he will repay those who hate him, and cleanse the land for his people.

That all gods worship Him means that the Gentile nations are also rejoicing; that is the way many other translations have interpreted it.

Running through the Song of Moses are two themes: God's faithfulness to His people and His judgment on His nation that has rejected Him. But in the end, there is a prophetic expectation that God will revenge the death of His people and bring all nations to rejoice in God.

This song is sung by those who have overcome the beast, and they are also singing the Song of the Lamb. In this new song, the destinies

REVELATION 15

of the elect of Israel and the Gentiles will be brought together for eternity. There can be only one Bride of Christ.

The Song of Moses mourns God's judgment on those who have fallen away. What happened to the Israelites will also happen to God's new chosen people: there will be an apostasy—falling away from God's ways. The Church and the Western civilisation have become fat because of God's blessings, but they have forgotten their Maker and the One who has blessed them.

It is striking that the New Testament story of the Church follows the trajectory of the Old Testament story of Israel. God chooses Israel. She is blessed. She rejects God. She is judged. Then God chooses the Gentiles. They are blessed. Many of them reject God. They are judged.

At this point, the harvest of salvation has already been gathered. The time to avenge the blood of God's servants has come.

The elect are in heaven where they stand "beside the sea of glass with harps of God in their hands". The true Church and the elect of Israel will have been taken up to heaven before the very final judgments of the earth.

Verse 8 ending the chapter says that:

> The temple was filled with smoke from the glory of God and from his power, and no one could enter the temple until the seven plagues of the seven angels were ended.

This indicates that for this time, God will forsake the earth, and no one has access to His presence. There will come a time when, because of God's wrath, His presence cannot be found on earth. Woe to those who will be on earth at that time!

REVELATION 16

Revelation 16 begins the account of the seven plagues of God's wrath. The access to God's temple is shut. God has left humanity orphaned. He no more restrains the evil that is taking place on earth, and consequently, the principle of cause and effect is fully operational. Humanity will reap what they have sown, as God has removed His mercy that has diluted the consequences of man's evil actions. But now humanity will reap the harvest of its own sin.

The first angel pours out his bowl on the land and on everyone who had worshipped the beast or his image. It is now evident that the beast and his image cannot be limited to the historical Roman Empire.

At this point, Babylon has already fallen, which means that the Roman Empire is gone—even when *Revelation 18* will account the second fall of Babylon.

It appears that *Revelation 16* reveals the judgment of the nations, whereas *Revelation 18* will reveal the judgment of the prostitute Church. They prophesy about the same period. This implies that the second beast has been at least partially severed from the first beast.

The earlier chapters of Revelation describe the Church and the empire coming together. In *Revelation 16-17*, the empire has separated from the Church.

The beast will metamorphose to take different shapes in different times, but it will remain the beast. Perhaps the different elements of the beast have different prominence in different times.

The beast, now separate from the Church, is still killing, raping, and murdering nations. It cannot deny its nature. And now it will turn

UNDERSTANDING REVELATION

its attention on the prostitute Church. No ruler has ever been able to tame the empire, but each empire has always pillaged and looted other nations. That is how the empires maintain their prominence. World history has not witnessed a singular empire that has not acquired and maintained their dominance without violence.

Looking at the woes in Revelation, the first woe is in *Revelation 8:13*, when one third of the earth has been struck.

The second woe takes place in *Revelation 11:14*, when God does something miraculous in the end-time Israel.

The third woe is linked to the judgment on Babylon, which will come in *Revelation 18*.

The three woes represent the three judgments in Revelation:

1. Judgment of humanity
2. Judgment of humanity because of Israel
3. Judgment of the prostitute Church.

These are the three end-time judgments. Israel will not be judged separately anymore, as she was already judged in the destruction of the Second Temple and the following exile. But the prostitute Church is yet to be judged.

The second angel pours out his bowl on the sea, and every living thing in the sea dies.

The third angel pours out his bowls on the springs and the rivers, and they become blood. *Verses 4-6* say:

> The third angel poured his bowl into the rivers and the springs of water, and they became blood. And I heard the angel of the waters say, "You are just, O Holy One, who are and were, for you have judged these things; because they shed the blood of saints and prophets, you have given them blood to drink. It is what they deserve!"

God will not judge His saints, but those who have shed their blood. His saints will already be in heaven. But because of His saints and the prophets, the rivers of the earth will run like blood.

The fourth angel pours out his bowl on the sun, and the sun is given power to scorch people with fire.

REVELATION 16

The fifth angel pours out his bowl on the throne of the beast, and his kingdom is plunged into darkness. People curse God because of their pains and sores.

The sixth angel pours out his bowl on the great river Euphrates, and its water is dried up to prepare the way for the kings of the East. Then three evil spirits that look like frogs come out of the mouth of the dragon, beast, and the false prophet. Now we can see that the second beast with two horns was a false prophet indeed.

The dragon is Satan, the beast is the man-made empire, and the false prophet is the false Church.

The true Church has been raptured, but that has left behind the earthly church institutions.

These mighty demons can perform miraculous signs, and they gather the kings for the battle in Armageddon on the great day of the God Almighty. Again, it is not clear whether the signs will be actual miracles, or if this merely indicates that what will happen will be energised by demonic power. The serpent offered Adam and Eve knowledge, so that they would become like gods, and this knowledge, accumulated by humanity, might take us to our destruction when demonically misused.

Revelation 16:15 reminds:

> Blessed is the one who stays awake and is clothed, not going about naked and exposed to shame.

Verse 15 reminds Christians that they don't need to experience these events.

The seventh angel pours out his bowl, and cities collapse because of the earthquake. Every island flees away, and no mountains are to be found, as the earth shakes under the final judgment. This speeds us to the end of judgments, and to the Second Coming of Jesus.

John refers to this as God remembering "Babylon the Great".

The seven bowls describe the fullness of the end-time judgment and destruction. In the end of *Revelation 16*, humanity will be cursing God because of the plagues. Because God cannot be found on earth at this time, the nations will remain unrepentant. It remains an enigma whether an individual person will be able to find God at this time.

Perhaps an individual can still find mercy. But God will not have mercy on the nations.

The Tenth Vision

REVELATION 17

Revelation 17 begins to explain the identity of Babylon the Great. Babylon the Great has already been destroyed, what follows is the explanation for her judgment. *Revelation 17* is not happening after the judgments of *Revelation 16* but simultaneously:

> Then one of the seven angels who had the seven bowls came and said to me, "Come, I will show you the judgment of the great whore who is seated on many waters, with whom the kings of the earth have committed fornication, and with the wine of whose fornication the inhabitants of the earth have become drunk." So he carried me away in the spirit into a wilderness, and I saw a woman sitting on a scarlet beast that was full of blasphemous names, and it had seven heads and ten horns. The woman was clothed in purple and scarlet, and adorned with gold and jewels and pearls, holding in her hand a golden cup full of abominations and the impurities of her fornication; and on her forehead was written a name, a mystery: "Babylon the great, mother of whores and of earth's abominations." And I saw that the woman was drunk with the blood of the saints and the blood of the witnesses to Jesus. When I saw her, I was greatly amazed. But the angel said to me, "Why are you so amazed? I will tell you the mystery of the woman, and of the beast with seven heads and ten horns that carries her. The beast that you saw was, and is not, and is about to ascend from the bottomless pit and go to destruction. And the inhabitants of the earth, whose names have not been written in the book of life from the foundation of the world, will be amazed when they see the beast, because it was and is not and is to come."

UNDERSTANDING REVELATION

Verse 6 says that Babylon the Great is a mystery, but that she is also the mother of prostitutes and of the abominations of the earth. This means that the prostitution will begin in Rome, but it will spread to the earth through her daughters.

The Old Testament prophets present Judah and Israel as two prostitutes. After the destruction of Israel, there was only one prostitute left, the Kingdom of Judah with Jerusalem as her capital.

Isaiah 1:21-23 laments the degenerate city, Jerusalem:

> How the faithful city has become a whore! She that was full of justice, righteousness lodged in her—but now murderers! Your silver has become dross, your wine is mixed with water. Your princes are rebels and companions of thieves. Everyone loves a bribe and runs after gifts. They do not defend the orphan, and the widow's cause does not come before them.

The angel carries John away into a desert, where a woman sits on a scarlet beast. Earlier on, there was another woman, Israel, in the wilderness. We can see how wilderness means separation from God for someone who is meant to be with Him. This is not Israel, but another woman.

So, Babylon the Great is another woman, not Israel, who should be married to God but has instead chosen to live in separation from Him. The woman, who has gathered gold, precious stones and pearls, is dressed in purple and scarlet, enjoying her wealth, has ended up in the wilderness, just like Israel, in pursuit of her luxuries.

The angel says that kings of the earth committed adultery with her. Only someone who is married can commit adultery, and it was because Israel was married to God that she was judged for her adultery.

In contrast, Revelation ends with yet another woman, the Bride of Christ, having the wedding party with the Lamb.

The woman sits on a scarlet beast that is covered with blasphemous names. It has seven heads and ten horns. It is clear from previous chapters that this beast is Rome. But now it has scarlet colour. It has metamorphosed into something new.

She has a golden cup in her hand, filled with abominable things and the filth of her adulteries. *Jeremiah 51:7* says:

REVELATION 17

> Babylon was a golden cup in the Lord's hand, making all the earth drunken; the nations drank of her wine, and so the nations went mad.

This woman is not Babylon, or Rome, but she has drunk from the golden cup of Babylon. Her forehead has the title: Mystery, Babylon the Great, the Mother of Prostitutes and of the Abominations of the Earth.

John sees that the woman is drunk with the blood of the saints. What is remarkable is that up to this point John has never been astonished. He has seen visions that we have been baffled by for centuries, and nothing seems to have confused him. But the prostitute riding on the beast astonishes him.

He has not been astonished at the persecution of the saints. He has not been astonished by the judgments. But now he is astonished.

Perhaps he is seeing something that he has not expected at all. The angel asks him why he is astonished and then begins to explain the mystery behind the woman.

We must be careful to separate the angel's explanation of what the beast is from the identity of the prostitute. After all, the beast is now purple, and the woman is now riding on it. By separating them we can discern two separate prophecies, one for the Early Church and another for the end-times.

The angel says that the beast the prostitute is riding on, the beast he saw, once was, now is not, but later, it will come out of the Abyss and go to his destruction.

Let us look at the explanation of the beast. The angel is calling for a mind with wisdom. The seven heads are the seven hills on which the woman sits—the seven hills of Rome.

He says that five have fallen, one is, the other has not yet come; but when he comes, he must remain for a little while. The beast who once was, and now is not, is an eighth king. He belongs to the seven and is going to his destruction.

When the angel calls for wisdom, what he means is that this explanation is not straightforward.

What is noteworthy is that the beast is an eighth king—who once was and now is not. This is the one moment when the beast is nearly

UNDERSTANDING REVELATION

fully identified with a person. At all other times in Revelation, the beast is the empire.

This identity of the eighth king is a riddle that would have been a lot easier to understand in John's time than today. The main purpose of the riddle is to connect John's revelation seamlessly with the vision about the beast in *Daniel 7*, and to provide continuity for it. So, knowing the exact time of when John received this explanation might not be necessary, as it works whether he received it during the rule of Vespasian, Titus, or Domitian, because it is there to bring the continuity between the Old and New Covenant prophecies. If you play "Who am I?" guessing game, the riddle is always presented to you in a present tense even when the person in question has already passed away.

According to the angel, there are seven kings, of which five have fallen. This connects us with the beast in *Revelation 13*.

These were the first ten emperors of Rome.

1. Augustus (31 BC–AD 14)
2. Tiberius (AD 14–37)
3. Caligula (AD 37–41)
4. Claudius (AD 41–54)
5. Nero (AD 54–68)
6. Galba (AD 68–69)
7. Otho (January–April, AD 69)
8. Aulus Vitellius (July–December, AD 69)
9. Vespasian (AD 69–79)
10. Titus (AD 79–81)

Caesar was not an emperor, so he is not counted. We must also remember that this was written in the time of the Flavian Dynasty, which included Vespasian, his son Titus and Titus's brother Domitian.

Galba, Otho and Vitellius, although acknowledged to be short-lived emperors during the Year of the Four Emperors by modern historiography, were in fact Vespasian's contenders to the throne, and they would not have been recognised as emperors during the Flavian Dynasty. So, the three horns that were removed by the

REVELATION 17

little horn in *Daniel 7* were self-declared emperors that tried to usurp the rule, but it was Vespasian who won the contest and became the ruler.

So, assuming that is the case, Vespasian who ruled in AD 69-79 would have been the sixth, Titus who ruled very briefly in AD 79-81 would have been the seventh, and Domitian who ruled in AD 81-96 would have been the eighth.

The beast who once was and now is not would then clearly be Domitian. Considering that Domitian was hailed as emperor before his father Vespasian, he would clearly fit the bill. But he would go to his destruction. The story of his premature inauguration by the troops would have been well known at the time. After all, it has even been preserved to us.

The angel's explanation links Revelation seamlessly with the Book of Daniel and provides prophetic continuity between the Old and the New Covenants. According to the angel, the ten horns are ten kings that have not yet received the kingdom, but who for one hour will receive authority as kings along the beast. These kings will make war against the Lamb, but the Lamb will overcome them.

John's vision repurposes the ten horns of Daniel's vision. The beast is still the same beast, the Roman Empire, but now the ten horns become future-oriented. Daniel's prophecy is now past; it is time to prophesy about the ten horns again.

Augustine of Hippo (AD 354-430), who lived soon after the persecution of Christians had ended in the Roman Empire, writes in Chapter 52 of *City of God*:

> I do not think, indeed, that what some have thought or may think is rashly said or believed, that until the time of Antichrist the Church of Christ is not to suffer any persecutions besides those she has already suffered—that is, *ten*—and that the eleventh and last shall be inflicted by Antichrist. They reckon as the first that made by Nero, the second by Domitian, the third by Trajan, the fourth by Antoninus, the fifth by Severus, the sixth by Maximin, the seventh by Decius, the eighth by Valerian, the ninth by Aurelian, the tenth by Diocletian and Maximian.

UNDERSTANDING REVELATION

Looking back, some of Augustine's contemporaries can discern ten seasons of persecution and conclude that there will be no more waves of persecution to come until the emergence of a final Antichrist.

Augustine does not seem to contest the calculation of ten waves of persecution. Now, I disagree with Augustine about the theory of an end-time Antichrist, but it seems reasonable to assume that he would be quite knowledgeable about the history of the Church under the Roman Empire.

According to *verse 12*, these are ten kings "who have not yet received a kingdom, but they are to receive authority as kings for one hour, together with the beast."

We must review our calculation, as these ten kings have not yet received authority, but in time of Revelation, Nero's rule had already passed. So, we cannot count Nero in the ten persecutions, but based on what John's explanation of who the eighth emperor is—Domitian —and that he had not ruled yet, we can include Domitian.

So, that would leave us with nine major waves of persecution. Where is the missing wave of persecution?

For some reason, Augustine and his contemporaries make one glaring omission, perhaps because that wave of persecution took place after Christianity had already taken a firm hold on the empire.

Emperor Flavius Claudius Iulianius (AD 361-363) is better known as Julian the Apostate. He renounced Christianity when he became the sole emperor and tried to reinstitute paganism. When Julian arrived in Antioch, the citizens went to meet him and welcome him with public prayers, as if he were god and shouted that a lucky star had risen over the East. But Julian, although he harmed Christians considerably, was not as violent a persecutor as many of his predecessors had been. But some of the persecution would have operated under the disguise of Christians being condemned for crimes rather than being persecuted for faith, and Christian sources name several dozen martyrs under Julian. (Teitler 2013, 263, 264, 267, 269)

What makes Julian the Apostate interesting is that he fulfils all the signs of the stereotypical end-time Antichrist—whilst ruling briefly on the fourth century.

Under Julian's reign, Christian teaching was restricted, and public pagan sacrifices abounded. Julian the Apostate even planned to

REVELATION 17

rebuild the temple in Jerusalem. But the work on the Temple Mount came to swift end when Julian died in the hands of the Persians. But its effects lingered in the Christian consciousness for years to come. Many Christian thinkers, such as Ambrosiaster, saw the Antichrist as the god of the gods of Rome after these events. (Hughes 2005, 33, 50)

In AD 363, not long before Julian left Antioch to launch his campaign against Persia, in keeping with his effort to foster religions other than Christianity, he ordered the Jewish temple rebuilt. Ammianus Marcellinus wrote this about the effort:

> Julian thought to rebuild at an extravagant expense the proud Temple once at Jerusalem, and committed this task to *Alypius of Antioch*. Alypius set vigorously to work, and was seconded by the *governor of the province*; when fearful balls of fire, breaking out near the foundations, continued their attacks, till the workmen, after repeated scorchings, could approach no more: and he gave up the attempt.

Julian the Apostate released the last onslaught of paganism against Christianity, and he left his mark on any later theories about the future Antichrist.

There is another vision about the Roman Empire in Daniel that is meaningful to us. In *Daniel 2*, the prophet sees a vision about a great statue that will be crushed by the Kingdom of God. This vision shows the empires of Babylon, Persia, Greece, and Rome with two legs.

There is an interesting development that takes place during the centuries when the ten persecutions took place. Initially, the emperors were all born in Rome. But eventually there were even former slaves that became emperors, as the ethnic Romans began to gradually lose control over their own empire.

In *Daniel 2*, the iron legs of the Roman empire become the feet of mix of clay and iron, made of weak and strong materials that do not mix.

Both John and Daniel refer to the same development. In *Daniel 2*, the Roman Empire grows two legs, and feet of iron and clay, but it is destroyed by the Rock. In *Revelation 17*, the saints will overcome the ten kings.

UNDERSTANDING REVELATION

Eventually, the Roman Empire was divided in two parts, the Eastern and the Western Roman Empire. The Western Roman Empire was dissolved, but the Eastern Roman Empire became the Byzantium that survived for another thousand years. But even the Western Roman Empire found some continuity in the Holy Roman Empire. So, the two legs and feet in Daniel's vision represent the division of the Roman Empire into two empires.

In John's prophecy about the ten kings, the saints will overcome the beast. This happens, and both the Byzantium and the Holy Roman Empire were Christian empires. But the consequences of this victory of saints are surprising, as this victory leads to the prostitution of the Church.

During these ten persecutions the Church began to modify her teachings and practice to make herself more acceptable to the Roman Empire. The first steps were taken in Ephesus where the Church began to link Mary with Artemis. This has shaped the whole Western Church and the Eastern Church in ways we find difficult to understand.

In her victory over the beast, the Church ends up riding on it. The destinies of the empire and the Church merge. But then something new will emerge. *Verses 15-18* say:

> And he said to me, "The waters that you saw, where the whore is seated, are peoples and multitudes and nations and languages. And the ten horns that you saw, they and the beast will hate the whore; they will make her desolate and naked; they will devour her flesh and burn her up with fire. For God has put it into their hearts to carry out his purpose by agreeing to give their kingdom to the beast, until the words of God will be fulfilled. The woman you saw is the great city that rules over the kings of the earth."

The waters where the prostitute sits are peoples, multitudes, nations, and languages. So, the prostitute has expanded herself into many nations. The second beast, the prostitute, came from the earth, whereas the first beast came from the sea of nations. Now the prostitute is seated on the sea of nations, but it is the first beast that she has been riding to get her there.

REVELATION 17

This describes the expansion of the Church into global Christendom and the aspects of it that have prostituted our faith. So, although, the prostitution begins from Rome, it will spread around the world.

The beast and the ten horns will hate the prostitute, and they will make her naked and destroy her. Why is that? At this point, the hatred is probably released because the saints are already in heaven. At this point, the prostitute is what is left of the Church.

This speaks also for the re-emergence of hatred against the Church by formerly Christianised nations in the end-times, specifically within the former territory of the Roman Empire. So, there will come a time in the end-times when the Church will be hated at her former heartland. But this also indicates some level of global attack against the Church led by the Western nations near the end of times.

But the Church that will be hated will be the prostitute Church that in earlier times found herself comfortable with the rulers and merchants of the nations.

The Eleventh Vision

REVELATION 18

If the great fall of the Old Testament was the fall of Israel, then the great fall of the New Testament must be the fall of the Church.

Revelation 18 follows the pattern of prophetic wailing of the Old Testament prophets over Jerusalem, only this time it is over Rome.

The Western civilisation built on the Roman Empire but spread with the help of the prostitute Church has been one of the great destroyers of all ages.

There have been many other destroyers before and after, but what makes our sin so grave is that we have done these atrocities in the name of Jesus—in the name of God of the Bible. We have defamed His Name in the nations.

The main bulk of the Old Testament prophecy predicts the destruction of the kingdoms of Israel and Judah, Jerusalem, and the temple because of their prostitution. In similar vein, the great destruction prophesied in the New Testament will be the destruction of the prostitute Church.

Paul writes in *Romans 2:24*:

> For, as it is written, "The name of God is blasphemed among the Gentiles because of you."

Ezekiel 36:22-23 says:

> Therefore say to the house of Israel, "Thus says the Lord God: 'It is not for your sake, O house of Israel, that I am about to act, but for the sake of my holy name, which you have profaned among the nations to which you came. I will sanctify my great

UNDERSTANDING REVELATION

name, which has been profaned among the nations, and which you have profaned among them; and the nations shall know that I am the Lord, says the Lord God, when through you I display my holiness before their eyes.'"

The name of God was first blasphemed because of Israel; in our time His name has often been blasphemed because of the Church.

In *verse 2*, an angel cries:

> Fallen, fallen is Babylon the great! It has become a dwelling place of demons, a haunt of every foul spirit.

Rather than being full of the Holy Spirit, the Church has become the dwelling place for demons!

Verse 3 begins to list her adulteries with the kings and the merchants of the world. This makes clear that the prostitution of the Church is firmly connected with the power and money the kings and merchants possess.

Verses 4-5 say:

> Come out of her, my people, so that you do not take part in her sins, and so that you do not share in her plagues; for her sins are heaped high as heaven, and God has remembered her iniquities.

It was impossible for the Christians to come out of the beast, the Roman Empire, hence they were asked to persevere. But it is possible for Gods' people to come out of Babylon the Great. Perhaps, in near future, before the end and before the Rapture, there will come a time when it will be impossible for God's people to remain in some institutions that we call churches; so deep will their compromise be. Many churches will become fully apostate.

In *Revelation 18*, she will be paid back double for her sins. It is the kings of the earth that share her luxury; it seems that she became even wealthier than many nations. Most of the items in the trading list are items which have been traded over centuries. Unlike with the symbolic parts of the visions, these items listed seem like a real purchased goods, including marble and incense,

REVELATION 18

which have been part of the traditional church buildings and worship for centuries.

The merchants of the earth mourn for her, as no one will buy their wares anymore, including the bodies and souls of men.

As we have learnt earlier, the modern banking system including the currency exchange system were partially created to cater for the needs of the Pope and the Church in the fourteenth century. (Parks 2006, 46-51)

But the sins of the Church run deep. For example, at some point, the King of England was a slaveowner, and the slaves were branded with the brand of the king. Christians might have brought the abolition of slavery, but before that, the Church endorsed it.

The Christian-endorsed military machine has invaded all parts of the world through the project of imperialism and committed horrendous atrocities. The crimes endorsed by the Church, if not for anything but by silence, are so many that they cannot be listed here, but for example, in Germany, large part of the Church was quiet when the Nazis exterminated millions of Jews, even when other church leaders were sent to prison and concentration camp for defending the Jews. And parts of the Church participated in the genocide in Rwanda. The price of colonialism, endorsed by the Church, can be counted in tens of millions of lives.

And all that time, much of the Church was quiet. Surely the sins of the Church must be recorded somewhere. And God has recorded them.

Verse 20 says that God has judged the Church for the way she treated the prophets and apostles. *Verses 21-24* say:

> Then a mighty angel took up a stone like a great millstone and threw it into the sea, saying, "With such violence Babylon the great city will be thrown down, and will be found no more; and the sound of harpists and minstrels and of flutists and trumpeters will be heard in you no more; and an artisan of any trade will be found in you no more; and the sound of the millstone will be heard in you no more; and the light of a lamp will shine in you no more; and the voice of bridegroom and bride will be heard in you no more; for your merchants were the magnates of the earth, and all nations were deceived by

your sorcery. And in you was found the blood of prophets and of saints, and of all who have been slaughtered on earth."

The judgment of the prostitute will come suddenly. It appears that she will be judged additionally via the nations and not just as part of the general end-time judgments. But these final verses of this chapter bring together the judgment of the prostitute and the judgment of the beast.

Did we think God did not see when the Church profaned His name over centuries? He did not ignore the sins of Israel and Judah but judged them. And although the judgment tarried, when it came, it came suddenly, and there was one generation that ended up paying for it on earth with others only paying for it in eternity.

From the beginning, the imperial Church began to shed blood, even the blood of the saints and prophets.

In AD 355, Emperor Constantius began to unite the divided Church at any cost. The Christian emperors replaced pagan sacrifice with Christian communion, and the empire was willing to use lethal force to get people to participate in it. So, the Holy Communion, which was supposed to unite the saints, became the reason to shed the blood of those that disagreed with the imperial Church. In the fourth and fifth centuries, Christian orthodoxy became an increasingly significant ideological underpinning of the Roman imperial state's claim to legitimacy. The boundary between secular and ecclesiastical spheres was rapidly eroding. Bishops began to act more and more like secular potentates. (Gaddis 2005)

For example, the Christian followers of Athanasius in the Alexandrian church were attacked by the imperial government in AD 356, as Emperor Constantius attempted to install a bishop of his liking. This is their account:

> While we were keeping vigil in the Lord's house, and engaged in our prayers, suddenly about midnight the most illustrious dux Syrianus attacked us and the church with many legions of soldiers armed with naked swords and javelins and other warlike instruments, and wearing helmets on their heads; and actually while we were praying, and while the lessons were being read, they broke down the doors. And when the doors

REVELATION 18

> were burst open by the violence of the multitude, he gave command, and some of them were shooting; others shouting, their weapons rattling, and their swords flashing in the light of the lamps; and forthwith virgins were being slain, many men trampled down, and falling over one another as the soldiers came upon them, and several were pierced with arrows and perished. Some of the soldiers also were betaking themselves to plunder, and were stripping the virgins, who were more afraid of being even touched by them than they were of death . . . And when they saw that many had perished, they gave orders to the soldiers to remove out of sight the bodies of the dead. But the most holy virgins who were left behind were buried in the tombs, having attained the glory of martyrdom in the time of the most religious Constantius. Deacons also were beaten with stripes even in the Lord's house, and were shut up there. Nor did matters stop even here; for after all this had happened, whosoever pleased broke open any door that he could, and searched, and plundered what was within. They entered even into those places which not even all Christians are allowed to enter. (ibid.)

The history of the Church against those considered to be heretics has been violent and written in the blood of the martyrs.

And the story of atrocities continues—for example, when the United States dropped an atomic bomb to Nagasaki in the end of the Second World War, it wiped out the centre of Catholic Christianity in Japan.

No wonder John was astonished. He could not have expected that the Church would participate in the slaughter of nations. Neither could he have anticipated that the blood of the prophets and saints could be found in the Church.

But Jesus said the same about Israel. He says in *Luke 11:47-51*:

> Woe to you! For you build the tombs of the prophets whom your ancestors killed. So you are witnesses and approve of the deeds of your ancestors; for they killed them, and you build their tombs. Therefore also the Wisdom of God said, "I will send them prophets and apostles, some of whom they will kill and persecute," so that this generation may be charged with

UNDERSTANDING REVELATION

the blood of all the prophets shed since the foundation of the world, from the blood of Abel to the blood of Zechariah, who perished between the altar and the sanctuary. Yes, I tell you, it will be charged against this generation.

There was one generation in Israel to whom the blood of the prophets was charged. It was the generation that came after Jesus. That generation saw the destruction of Jerusalem, the Second Temple, and the slaughter of over million Jesus, resulting in the exile of the Jews. There will come a time when something similarly catastrophic will happen to the remains of Christendom.

The Twelfth Vision

REVELATION 19

Revelation 19 begins with a celebration in heaven, as the saved are celebrating the judgment of the prostitute and the avenging of the blood of God's servants.

The Song of Moses, in *Deuteronomy 32:43*, says:

> Praise, O heavens, his people, worship him, all you gods! For he will avenge the blood of his children, and take vengeance on his adversaries; he will repay those who hate him, and cleanse the land for his people.

Isaiah 34 prophesies the judgment of the nations; taken together, God is finally avenging the blood of His children, and it is the nations that are the target of His wrath. The sins of the prostitute must he horrendous in the sight of heaven.

Then the twenty-four elders and the four living beings worship God and confess that His judgments are just.

Verses 7-8 say:

> Let us rejoice and exult and give him the glory, for the marriage of the Lamb has come, and his bride has made herself ready; to her it has been granted to be clothed with fine linen, bright and pure—for the fine linen is the righteous deeds of the saints.

The judgement of the prostitute is contrasted with the joy of expecting the wedding. The horrendous fate of the prostitute is made clear. She was supposed to attend the wedding; instead, she has been judged with the beast.

UNDERSTANDING REVELATION

In *verse 10*, John prostrates in front of the angel to worship him, but the angel responds:

> You must not do that! I am a fellow servant with you and your comrades who hold the testimony of Jesus. Worship God! For the testimony of Jesus is the spirit of prophecy.

This is John, the disciple that loved Jesus, and yet he makes a mistake of attempting to worship an angel. So easily can our spiritual experiences become idolatrous.

What does it mean that the testimony of Jesus is the spirit of prophecy? That the purpose of prophecy is to testify about Jesus. The testimony of Jesus is that He is the Lamb but also the Lord, and there is no other.

Then the rider on the white horse arrives. He is called the King of Kings and Lord of Lords, and He will strike down the nations with the sword of His mouth, and He will rule the nations with a rod of iron. He is called The Word of God.

Psalm 2:7-9 says:

> I will tell of the decree of the Lord: He said to me, "You are my son; today I have begotten you. Ask of me, and I will make the nations your heritage, and the ends of the earth your possession. You shall break them with a rod of iron, and dash them in pieces like a potter's vessel."

Isaiah 11:4-6 predicts after prophesying about the first coming of the Messiah and him having the seven spirits of God:

> He shall strike the earth with the rod of his mouth, and with the breath of his lips he shall kill the wicked. Righteousness shall be the belt around his waist, and faithfulness the belt around his loins. The wolf shall live with the lamb, the leopard shall lie down with the kid, the calf and the lion and the fatling together, and a little child shall lead them.

Revelation presents the Second Coming of Jesus as the fulfilment of the messianic prophecies that will usher in the Kingdom of Peace.

REVELATION 19

There is so much symbolism in this prophetic language that it is difficult to tell what will happen exactly, and what this rule of the Messiah will look like. But the main point seems to be that hostility brought by sin, first by the sin of angels and then by man, is removed from the earth.

At this point the armies of the beast are defeated; this is the battle of the Lord against Gog and Magog.

Ezekiel 39:11-16 prophesies:

> On that day I will give to Gog a place for burial in Israel, the Valley of the Travelers east of the sea; it shall block the path of the travelers, for there Gog and all his horde will be buried; it shall be called the Valley of Hamon-gog. Seven months the house of Israel shall spend burying them, in order to cleanse the land. All the people of the land shall bury them; and it will bring them honor on the day that I show my glory, says the Lord God. They will set apart men to pass through the land regularly and bury any invaders who remain on the face of the land, so as to cleanse it; for seven months they shall make their search. As the searchers pass through the land, anyone who sees a human bone shall set up a sign by it, until the buriers have buried it in the Valley of Hamon-gog. (A city Hamonah is there also.) Thus they shall cleanse the land.

This prophecy implies that after the battle the land will be purified, and this will pave the way to the account of the Millennial Kingdom in *Revelation 20*.

Joel 3:1-3, which accounts for the same battle, gives us the reason for this carnage:

> For then, in those days and at that time, when I restore the fortunes of Judah and Jerusalem, I will gather all the nations and bring them down to the valley of Jehoshaphat, and I will enter into judgment with them there, on account of my people and my heritage Israel, because they have scattered them among the nations. They have divided my land, and cast lots for my people, and traded boys for prostitutes, and sold girls for wine, and drunk it down.

UNDERSTANDING REVELATION

This is the judgment of the nations for scattering the Jews over the last two millennia. *Zechariah 12:10-14* says:

> And I will pour out a spirit of compassion and supplication on the house of David and the inhabitants of Jerusalem, so that, when they look on the one whom they have pierced, they shall mourn for him, as one mourns for an only child, and weep bitterly over him, as one weeps over a firstborn. On that day the mourning in Jerusalem will be as great as the mourning for Hadad-rimmon in the plain of Megiddo. The land shall mourn, each family by itself; the family of the house of David by itself, and their wives by themselves; the family of the house of Nathan by itself, and their wives by themselves; the family of the house of Levi by itself, and their wives by themselves; the family of the Shimeites by itself, and their wives by themselves; and all the families that are left, each by itself, and their wives by themselves.

This is the time when Israel will realise that they did miss the first coming of the Messiah, and they will mourn.

At this point the beast and the false prophet are thrown into hellfire for eternity. *Verse 21* says:

> And the rest were killed by the sword of the rider on the horse, the sword that came from his mouth; and all the birds were gorged with their flesh.

It is the Word of God coming from the mouth of Jesus that kills the rest of the armies of the beast and the kings of the earth.

Again, there is so much symbolism in this book that it is difficult to see whether these forces of the beast will in fact see the heavenly armies. It is possible that they will only see the King of Kings at their death and that some other, more earthly forces, will in fact appear to execute this judgment.

An important part of Revelation is arranging the chronology of the Old Testament prophecy in the right sequence. In *Revelation 19*, we can see the end-time events prophesied in the Old Testament rearranged and sequenced so that they fit the New Covenant's vision of Jesus's return.

The Thirteenth Vision

REVELATION 20

Revelation 20 continues the story from *Revelation 19*. The devil is thrown into the pit by an angel for a thousand years. It takes only one angel to do that, which indicates that Lucifer might have never been the most powerful angel in heaven before his fall. But until now he has been protected by God's special exemption, so that he will be able to fulfil his purpose. *Isaiah 27:1* prophesies:

> On that day the Lord with his cruel and great and strong sword will punish Leviathan the fleeing serpent, Leviathan the twisting serpent, and he will kill the dragon that is in the sea.

For a thousand years, the devil will be kept from deceiving the nations. This is the time of the Millennial Kingdom.

There are three predominant views of the Millennium. Premillennialism believes that the Millennium will occur at the Second Coming of Christ, postmillennialism that it will occur toward the end of the church age, and amillennialism that it started at Jesus's resurrection and will end at His final coming. (Beale 1999, 356)

The problem with both postmillennial and amillennial view is that according to Revelation, Satan is released after imprisonment, and we have not seen him imprisoned yet. Also, the trouble any interpreter faces is that, even when there are many Old Testament prophecies about the rule of the Messiah on earth, *Revelation 20* is the only passage in the Bible that prophesies a thousand-year rule of Christ on earth. Many scholars have tried to establish where the thousand years might come from.

UNDERSTANDING REVELATION

Psalm 90:4 says:

> For a thousand years in your sight are like yesterday when it is past, or like a watch in the night.

The scholars that do not want to assign Millennialism to Zoroastrian influences from Persia take Psalm 90:4 to be the most likely reference point.

In Revelation, the Millennial Kingdom functions as a transition stage between life on earth and the time when heaven and earth are made new. The Old Testament is full of prophecies about Israel's restoration, and Revelation presents the Millennial Kingdom as fulfilment of these prophecies, because these prophecies do not promise a heavenly kingdom but a kingdom on earth.

Isaiah 4:2-6 says:

> On that day the branch of the Lord shall be beautiful and glorious, and the fruit of the land shall be the pride and glory of the survivors of Israel. Whoever is left in Zion and remains in Jerusalem will be called holy, everyone who has been recorded for life in Jerusalem, once the Lord has washed away the filth of the daughters of Zion and cleansed the bloodstains of Jerusalem from its midst by a spirit of judgment and by a spirit of burning. Then the Lord will create over the whole site of Mount Zion and over its places of assembly a cloud by day and smoke and the shining of a flaming fire by night. Indeed over all the glory there will be a canopy. It will serve as a pavilion, a shade by day from the heat, and a refuge and a shelter from the storm and rain.

Isaiah 61:5-6 says:

> Strangers shall stand and feed your flocks, foreigners shall till your land and dress your vines; but you shall be called priests of the Lord, you shall be named ministers of our God; you shall enjoy the wealth of the nations, and in their riches you shall glory.

Ezekiel 37:22-28 says:

REVELATION 20

Thus says the Lord God: "I will take the people of Israel from the nations among which they have gone, and will gather them from every quarter, and bring them to their own land. I will make them one nation in the land, on the mountains of Israel; and one king shall be king over them all. Never again shall they be two nations, and never again shall they be divided into two kingdoms. They shall never again defile themselves with their idols and their detestable things, or with any of their transgressions. I will save them from all the apostasies into which they have fallen, and will cleanse them. Then they shall be my people, and I will be their God. My servant David shall be king over them; and they shall all have one shepherd. They shall follow my ordinances and be careful to observe my statutes. They shall live in the land that I gave to my servant Jacob, in which your ancestors lived; they and their children and their children's children shall live there forever; and my servant David shall be their prince forever. I will make a covenant of peace with them; it shall be an everlasting covenant with them; and I will bless them and multiply them, and will set my sanctuary among them forevermore. My dwelling place shall be with them; and I will be their God, and they shall be my people. Then the nations shall know that I the LORD sanctify Israel, when my sanctuary is among them forevermore."

Zechariah 8:1-3 says:

The word of the Lord of hosts came to me, saying: "Thus says the Lord of hosts: I am jealous for Zion with great jealousy, and I am jealous for her with great wrath. Thus says the Lord: I will return to Zion, and will dwell in the midst of Jerusalem; Jerusalem shall be called the faithful city, and the mountain of the Lord of hosts shall be called the holy mountain."

So, the Millennial Kingdom represents the faithfulness of God to each one of His promises. But this extends beyond God's promises to Israel and even back to Adam and Eve.

After the Fall in Genesis, Adam and the first generations are told to have lived nearly a thousand years before God began to shorten their lives. Thereby, the Millennial Kingdom is also presented as the fulfilment of God's commandment for human beings to multiply

UNDERSTANDING REVELATION

and cultivate the land: to make the whole earth like the Garden of Eden. A thousand years is the length of the perfect life God had intended for humans, but this project was disrupted because the devil was given entrance to the Garden, and he deceived Adam and Eve.

This time, Satan is locked in hell for the duration of the perfect human life and then released in the end of it.

But is this Millennial Kingdom a real kingdom on earth, or is it here simply to demonstrate symbolically that God will fulfil every promise He has made to humanity?

What is fascinating is that the Millennial Kingdom appears not to be part of John's vision but part of his explanation. In *verse 4* he "sees" the thrones, and in *verse 11* he sees a "great white throne", but apart from the element of binding Satan and locking him up for a thousand years whilst the saints reign, the rest appears to recount the Old Testament prophecies.

There are three main elements in Revelation, and we must be careful when we transition between them:
- the visions John saw and their explanations by Jesus or by angels
- the references to the Old Testament prophecy
- John's own explanations.

So, there is a possibility that the Millennial Kingdom serves as John's explanation for how the unfulfilled prophecies of the Old Testament will be fulfilled. That does not mean that what John describes will not be fulfilled, only that perhaps even John does not fully understand what the fulfilment of those prophecies will look like.

In the beginning of the Millennial Kingdom, there are thrones given to some, and they are given authority to judge. These thrones are given for "the souls of those who had been beheaded for their testimony to Jesus and for the word of God." As a Roman citizen, the apostle Paul would have been beheaded at his martyrdom, but this is also a fitting reference point to the many martyrs that have been beheaded through the centuries, most recently by the Islamic extremists. According to Revelation, only those came to life and reigned with Christ for a thousand years; the rest of the dead did not come back to life until the thousand years were ended.

This is the first resurrection. It might seem that only the ones who

REVELATION 20

have been martyred will rise for a thousand years. But throughout Revelation, the focus has been on the martyred as the representation of the sufferings of all Christians.

According to the New Testament teaching, it is not only martyrs who will rule. But it is also imperative to understand that the reigning with Christ does not necessarily mean reigning in a kingdom that would be visible on earth but reigning with Christ in the heavenlies.

The first resurrection is the resurrection of the Christians.

After the thousand years, Satan will be released from the pit, and he will come out to deceive the nations at the four corners of the earth, Gog, and Magog, and they will gather against Jerusalem.

But the fire will come from heaven and consume them, and the devil will be thrown into the lake of fire, where the beast and the false prophet are already waiting for him.

This does not look like much of a battle, and Jesus will get rid of Gog and Magog quickly.

Are there two end-time battles around Jerusalem, one in the beginning and one in the end of a Millennial Kingdom?

Will there be a Millennial Kingdom on earth? That will be one of the few mysteries in Revelation we will be unable to solve before the time referred to as the Millennial Kingdom arrives.

But when the saints will rule, they will not be ruling like alien spiritual beings landing on earth, but they will rule in heaven. So, if there will be a Millennial Kingdom on earth, it seems that the heavenly reality will be separated from the earthly reality and largely invisible to humanity.

At this point, both the dead and the death itself are judged. This is a fulfilment of Old Testament prophecies:

Isaiah 26:19 says:

> Your dead shall live, their corpses shall rise. O dwellers in the dust, awake and sing for joy! For your dew is a radiant dew, and the earth will give birth to those long dead.

Again, this resurrection does not mean that people will somehow regain their already rotten bodies. That would be a zombie resurrection! And they have not been asleep through that time. But God cannot wait to receive the saints; that is why they are resurrected first. *Matthew 16:27* says:

> For the Son of Man is to come with his angels in the glory of his Father, and then he will repay everyone for what has been done.

What are the criteria of the judgment? Is this final judgment there just to send people to hell, as the Christians have been raised in the first resurrection?

This would mean that the only way to be saved would be to hear the gospel and to respond to it.

We have already looked at Jesus's description of the Last Judgment in *Matthew 25:31-46*, where the nations are judged by how they have treated those who were hungry, thirsty, strangers, naked, sick or in prison.

I do not pretend to understand the intricacies of the Last Judgment. But these verses from Matthew give me assurance that, indeed, God's judgments are fair. We must remember that He is the final judge and that our theology is not the final arbiter of truth. God is. But that does not mean any kind of universal salvation. Far from it. Jesus is still the only way to salvation. But God's judgment is God's judgment and not our judgment.

The fairness of God's judgment on those who never heard the gospel before they died is something the apostles had to grapple with, as the first-generation Christians would have asked them the question. Peter writes in *1 Peter 3:18-19*:

> He was put to death in the flesh, but made alive in the spirit, in which also he went and made a proclamation to the spirits in prison.

Paul writes in *1 Corinthians 15:29*:

> Otherwise, what will those people do who receive baptism on behalf of the dead? If the dead are not raised at all, why are people baptized on their behalf?

REVELATION 20

Peter does not say whether Jesus's preaching made any difference to the eternal state of those who disobeyed in time of Noah. Neither does it say that Paul condoned the practice of being baptised on behalf of the dead. But these verses illustrate that what happens to those who died without hearing the good news has always been a burning question in the Church. It is the main reason why the Church began baptising infant children.

To recap, the Millennial Kingdom seems to be presented to fulfil the prophecies about Israel and to give humanity an opportunity to one perfect life without the influence of Satan. That much seems to be clear. But any further speculation about what will happen will probably miss the mark. In the beginning of the Millennial Kingdom, Satan will be bound, until he will be released to deceive the nations. After that, he will be thrown in the lake of fire. The difficulty with this is that there are no other reference points to this binding and releasing of Satan in the Bible, so what will happen exactly remains partially an enigma.

In the end of *Revelation 20*, the outcome of the second resurrection is that those whose names are not in the Book of Life will be thrown in the lake of fire. And these people will be judged according to their works whereas the ones participating in the first resurrection will be judged according to the finished work of Christ on the cross.

It seems that at this point there is some checking on whether people's names are in the Book of Life or not. That leaves the question whether someone who is raised in the second resurrection can in fact be saved.

There has been a lot of speculation about the nature of hell over the centuries. I am not going to repeat it here. It is enough to say that it is the place of full separation from God and the presence of a multitude of demons. In my ministry, I have had to face plenty of spiritual warfare, and I can testify that without the presence of God, it can sometimes feel that the demonic beings might be able to rip your soul apart. What we know is that if God is love, it will be a loveless place, as all love in the universe originates from God. Some believe in the annihilation of the damned souls in hell. It is hard to see how that would be the case, at least according to the prophecies of Jesus and Revelation that do refer to eternal suffering.

UNDERSTANDING REVELATION

It was partially for "humanitarian" reasons that the Catholic Church introduced the doctrine of the Purgatory, which means temporary suffering in eternity, after which the tormented will eventually be released into heaven. There is no biblical evidence or reference point to Purgatory at all. It appears that the Last Judgment will have final consequences.

The Fourteenth Vision

REVELATION 21

Revelation 21 begins with a beautiful description of New Jerusalem. The first heaven and the first earth have passed away, and New Jerusalem descends from heaven like a bride prepared for her husband.

A loud voice says in *verses 3-4*:

> See, the home of God is among mortals. He will dwell with them; they will be his peoples, and God himself will be with them; he will wipe every tear from their eyes. Death will be no more; mourning and crying and pain will be no more, for the first things have passed away.

New Jerusalem is not a return to Eden but God's original plan. It is a city rather than a garden. And the city is the Bride. Or put another way, the Bride is a city—a community. So, God has prepared His people for the wedding. This descending from heaven symbolises that this city is entirely made in heaven, not that there would be some earthly city partially made in heaven. The division between the earth and heaven has disappeared. Heaven has absorbed earth. God's Kingdom has fully come. Or looking at it the other way, we have fully entered God's Kingdom.

Isaiah 61:10 prophesies:

> I will greatly rejoice in the Lord, my whole being shall exult in my God; for he has clothed me with the garments of salvation, he has covered me with the robe of righteousness, as a bridegroom decks himself with a garland, and as a bride adorns herself with her jewels.

UNDERSTANDING REVELATION

The marriage between God and His people is now being consumed. Heaven is the place of the greatest intimacy and absence of separation between man and God.

We often get God completely wrong. Yes, He is the Holy God. Yes, He hates sin. But He hates sin, because it separates us from Him and obstructs the intimate relationship He wants to enjoy with us. The metaphor He has chosen to describe about us coming together is the wedding party and the wedding night between the husband and the wife. And He is not embarrassed to call us His Bride.

Isaiah 25:6-10 prophesies:

> On this mountain the Lord of hosts will make for all peoples a feast of rich food, a feast of well-aged wines, of rich food filled with marrow, of well-aged wines strained clear. And he will destroy on this mountain the shroud that is cast over all peoples, the sheet that is spread over all nations; he will swallow up death forever. Then the Lord God will wipe away the tears from all faces, and the disgrace of his people he will take away from all the earth, for the Lord has spoken. It will be said on that day, Lo, this is our God; we have waited for him, so that he might save us. This is the Lord for whom we have waited; let us be glad and rejoice in his salvation. For the hand of the Lord will rest on this mountain.

We can see how Revelation explains the Old Testament prophecy in the light of Jesus. He has made all things new. It is done. This is the end of the story that He has begun. Perhaps it is a beginning of a new story that we will not hear until we meet Him.

But we are not only His Bride. We are also His children. Every metaphor of love is needed to explain the affection He feels for us. Also, everything that has disunited people on earth will be removed. Not only we get to experience God in an intimate way; we will also get to know human beings in a more intimate way than on earth. This might be one of the reasons why the only marriage in heaven is between God and His Bride.

I do not believe that heaven will be holy in the religious sense; it will be a place full of holy life beyond our imagination of what life can be.

REVELATION 21

When I was young, I detested the idea of heaven, as I did not want to end up as a pillar in the temple of God. That seemed to me like a very boring way to spend my eternity. But heaven will be full of life.

Isaiah 65:17-18-25 prophesies:

> For I am about to create new heavens and a new earth; the former things shall not be remembered or come to mind. But be glad and rejoice forever in what I am creating; for I am about to create Jerusalem as a joy, and its people as a delight. I will rejoice in Jerusalem, and delight in my people; no more shall the sound of weeping be heard in it, or the cry of distress. No more shall there be in it an infant that lives but a few days, or an old person who does not live out a lifetime; for one who dies at a hundred years will be considered a youth, and one who falls short of a hundred will be considered accursed. They shall build houses and inhabit them; they shall plant vineyards and eat their fruit. They shall not build and another inhabit; they shall not plant and another eat; for like the days of a tree shall the days of my people be, and my chosen shall long enjoy the work of their hands. They shall not labor in vain, or bear children for calamity; for they shall be offspring blessed by the Lord—and their descendants as well. Before they call I will answer, while they are yet speaking I will hear. The wolf and the lamb shall feed together, the lion shall eat straw like the ox; but the serpent—its food shall be dust! They shall not hurt or destroy on all my holy mountain, says the Lord.

There is a strong element of longevity but a distinct lack of eternal life in this prophecy. Similarly, it seems that Revelation places the Millennial Kingdom as a transition point between life on earth and eternity.

Then the angel who had carried one of bowls with the seven last judgments shows John the Bride, the wife of the Lamb, in detail. It has twelve gates with the names of Israel's tribes, and the wall of the city has twelve foundations, and on them are the twelve names of the twelve apostles of the Lamb. The angel measures the city and shows how it is pure gold, and how the walls of the city are adorned with twelve jewels.

UNDERSTANDING REVELATION

In one sense, this is a radical reworking of Ezekiel's vision of the perfect temple. John has read the whole inside of the scroll. He has seen not just a shadow of things to come but the things that are coming.

There is no temple in the city as the temple is God Himself.

We have encountered the twelve precious stones earlier in *Exodus 28:15-30*:

> You shall make a breastpiece of judgment, in skilled work; you shall make it in the style of the ephod; of gold, of blue and purple and crimson yarns, and of fine twisted linen you shall make it. It shall be square and doubled, a span in length and a span in width. You shall set in it four rows of stones. A row of carnelian, chrysolite, and emerald shall be the first row; and the second row a turquoise, a sapphire, and a moonstone; and the third row a jacinth, an agate, and an amethyst; and the fourth row a beryl, an onyx, and a jasper; they shall be set in gold filigree. There shall be twelve stones with names corresponding to the names of the sons of Israel; they shall be like signets, each engraved with its name, for the twelve tribes. You shall make for the breastpiece chains of pure gold, twisted like cords; and you shall make for the breastpiece two rings of gold, and put the two rings on the two edges of the breastpiece. You shall put the two cords of gold in the two rings at the edges of the breastpiece; the two ends of the two cords you shall attach to the two settings, and so attach it in front to the shoulder-pieces of the ephod. You shall make two rings of gold, and put them at the two ends of the breastpiece, on its inside edge next to the ephod. You shall make two rings of gold, and attach them in front to the lower part of the two shoulder-pieces of the ephod, at its joining above the decorated band of the ephod. The breastpiece shall be bound by its rings to the rings of the ephod with a blue cord, so that it may lie on the decorated band of the ephod, and so that the breastpiece shall not come loose from the ephod. So Aaron shall bear the names of the sons of Israel in the breastpiece of judgment on his heart when he goes into the holy place, for a continual remembrance before the Lord. In the breastpiece of judgment you shall put the Urim and the Thummim, and they shall be on Aaron's heart when he goes in before the Lord; thus Aaron shall bear the judgment of the Israelites on his heart before the Lord continually.

REVELATION 21

Not only is New Jerusalem the wife of the Lamb and the children of God; she is also the priest wearing the High Priest's breastpiece in the Holy of Holies. Looking back at *Revelation 1*, Jesus was not wearing the breastpiece, and it has now become New Jerusalem's foundation.

Isaiah 54 prophesies:

> O afflicted one, storm-tossed, and not comforted, I am about to set your stones in antimony, and lay your foundations with sapphires. I will make your pinnacles of rubies, your gates of jewels, and all your wall of precious stones.

Isaiah 60:19-20 prophesies:

> The sun shall no longer be your light by day, nor for brightness shall the moon give light to you by night; but the Lord will be your everlasting light, and your God will be your glory. Your sun shall no more go down, or your moon withdraw itself; for the Lord will be your everlasting light, and your days of mourning shall be ended.

In many ways, this description of heaven brings together various Old Testament prophecies regarding Israel's salvation, but it transports them into a new framework of eternal salvation. Again, we must remember that we are reading highly symbolic language, and one thing is certain: when we will get there, we will all be surprised.

Jesus says in *John 14:1-3:*

> Do not let your hearts be troubled. Believe in God, believe also in me. In my Father's house there are many dwelling places. If it were not so, would I have told you that I go to prepare a place for you? And if I go and prepare a place for you, I will come again and will take you to myself, so that where I am, there you may be also.

There is a thought I have pondered for a while: what if the mansion Jesus is preparing for us in heaven is ourselves? Then our reward in heaven will be that whatever we have done in Christ will be made manifest. After all, if the temple of God in heaven is God Himself,

UNDERSTANDING REVELATION

and we will be living in His intimate presence through eternity, where will we be living?

REVELATION 22

In *Revelation 22*, the angel shows John the river of water of life, flowing from the throne of God and of the Lamb; on both sides of the river is the Tree of Life. The name of God will be on the foreheads of God's servants, and they will see Him face to face.

So, there is not just one Tree of Life but two! This is not a return to Paradise, but for human beings, there will be three sources of life—reflecting the triune nature of God.

Ezekiel 47:1-2 prophesies:

> Then he brought me back to the entrance of the temple; there, water was flowing from below the threshold of the temple toward the east (for the temple faced east); and the water was flowing down from below the south end of the threshold of the temple, south of the altar. Then he brought me out by way of the north gate, and led me around on the outside to the outer gate that faces toward the east; and the water was coming out on the south side.

But Ezekiel's temple was at least partially an idealised earthly temple with some aspects of the heavenly temple. But this is heaven, and it is far superior to Ezekiel's idealised temple that the Jews would have been able to build had they been able to fulfil the Law.

Zechariah 14:6-9 prophesies:

> On that day there shall not be either cold or frost. And there shall be continuous day (it is known to the Lord), not day and not night, for at evening time there shall be light. On that day

living waters shall flow out from Jerusalem, half of them to the eastern sea and half of them to the western sea; it shall continue in summer as in winter. And the Lord will become king over all the earth; on that day the Lord will be one and his name one.

It seems that the Old Testament prophets have tried to interpret what they had seen through the shadows—through the Old Testament structures and institutions, and God has allowed them to do it. But John has now reinterpreted the symbols in the full light of the Lamb.

Verses 6-7 say:

> And he said to me, "These words are trustworthy and true, for the Lord, the God of the spirits of the prophets, has sent his angel to show his servants what must soon take place. See, I am coming soon! Blessed is the one who keeps the words of the prophecy of this book."

Verse 8 tells again that John was about to worship an angel; this seems more like a reminder about not doing that rather than a second attempt to do that.

Verse 10 says:

> Do not seal up the words of the prophecy of this book, for the time is near.

Verses 16-20 say:

> It is I, Jesus, who sent my angel to you with this testimony for the churches. I am the root and the descendant of David, the bright morning star. The Spirit and the bride say, "Come." And let everyone who hears say, "Come." And let everyone who is thirsty come. Let anyone who wishes take the water of life as a gift. I warn everyone who hears the words of the prophecy of this book: if anyone adds to them, God will add to that person the plagues described in this book; if anyone takes away from the words of the book of this prophecy, God will take away that person's share in the tree of life and in the holy city, which are described in this book. The one who testifies to these things says, "Surely I am coming soon." Amen. Come, Lord Jesus!

REVELATION 22

Revelation ends with the expectation of the Lord's coming.

In this book I have done my best to follow the clear principles of interpretation that Revelation itself gives to us whilst taking full benefit from historical research. That so much of Revelation can be explained today means that we have already entered the end-times.

I will have got some things wrong; that is for certain. Nevertheless, I hope that this book will help you in your own study of Revelation. And if you in some respects come to slightly different conclusions, it is no bother to me. But hopefully, this book has helped you to fall in love with God's Word and with the Lamb.

My final response to Revelation has always been, "*Maranatha!*" It is Aramaic, and it means, "Our Lord, come!"

BIBLIOGRAPHY

Aasgaard, Reidar. 'Among Gentiles, Jews, and Christians: Formation of Christian Identity in Melito of Sardis'. In *Religious Rivalries and the Struggle for Success in Sardis and Smyrna*, 156–74. Wilfred Laurier Univ. Press, 2005.

Ascough, Richard S. *Religious Rivalries and the Struggle for Success in Sardis and Smyrna*. Wilfrid Laurier Univ. Press, 2006.

Bailey, Kenneth E. *Paul Through Mediterranean Eyes: Cultural Studies in 1 Corinthians*. S.l.: SPCK Publishing, 2011.

Banducci, Laura M. 'A Tessera Lusoria from Gabii and the Afterlife of Roman Gaming'. *Herom* 4, no. 2 (November 2015): 199–221.

Beale, Gregory K. *John's Use of the Old Testament in Revelation*. A&C Black, 1999.

Carroll, Michael P. *The Cult of the Virgin Mary: Psychological Origins*. Princeton University Press, 1992.

Dunn, James D. G. *Beginning from Jerusalem: Christianity in the Making*. Wm. B. Eerdmans Publishing, 2009.

Eurell, John-Christian. *Peter's Legacy in Early Christianity: The Appropriation and Use of Peter's Authority in the First Three Centuries*. BoD—Books on Demand, 2020.

Filiu, Jean-Pierre. *Apocalypse in Islam*. University of California Press, 2011.

Friedrich, Nestor Paulo. 'Adapt or Resist? A Socio-Political Reading of Revelation 2.18-29'. *Journal for the Study of the New Testament* 25, no. 2 (1 December 2002): 185–21.

Friesen, Steven J. 'Satan's Throne, Imperial Cults and the Social

Settings of Revelation'. *Journal for the Study of the New Testament* 27, no. 3 (2005): 351–73.

Gabrielson, Timothy A. 'A Pagan Prophetess of the Jewish God: Religious Identity and Hellenization in the Third Sibyl'. *Journal for the Study of the Pseudepigrapha* 24, no. 3 (1 March 2015): 213–33.

Gadamer, Hans-Georg. *Truth and Method*. A&C Black, 2013.

Gaddis, Michael. *There Is No Crime for Those Who Have Christ: Religious Violence in the Christian Roman Empire*. 1st ed. University of California Press, 2005.

Gaston, Lloyd. 'Jewish Communities in Sardis and Smyrna'. In *Religious Rivalries and the Struggle for Success in Sardis and Smyrna*, 17–24. Ontaria: Wilfred Laurier University Press, 2006.

Hemer, Colin J. *The Letters to the Seven Churches of Asia in Their Local Setting*. W.B. Eerdmans Pub., 2001.

Herbert B. Huffmon. 'The Oracular Process: Delphi and the Near East'. *Vetus Testamentum* 57, no. 4 (2007): 449–60.

Horsley, G. H. R., and J. M. Luxford. 'Pagan Angels in Roman Asia Minor: Revisiting the Epigraphic Evidence.' *Anatolian Studies* 66 (2016): 141–83.

Hosang, F. J. E. Boddens. *Establishing Boundaries: Christian-Jewish Relations in Early Council Texts and the Writings of Church Fathers*. Brill, 2010.

Hughes, Kevin L. *Constructing Antichrist: Paul, Biblical Commentary, and the Development of Doctrine in the Early Middle Ages*. CUA Press, 2005.

Kierkegaard, Søren. *Kierkegaard's Writings, XXI, Volume 21: For Self-Examination/Judge for Yourself!* Princeton University Press, 1990.

Koester, Craig R. 'Revelation's Visionary Challenge to Ordinary Empire'. *Interpretation* 63, no. 1 (1 January 2009): 5–18.

Koester, Craig R. 'Roman Slave Trade and the Critique of Babylon in Revelation 18', 2008., 22.

Koester, Craig R. 'The Message to Laodicea and the Problem of Its Local Context: A Study of the Imagery in Rev 3.14–22'. *New Testament Studies* 49, no. 3 (July 2003): 407–24.

BIBLIOGRAPHY

Lampe, Peter. "Traces of Peter Veneration in Roman Archaeology." 273-317. In *Peter in Early Christianity*. Ed. by Helen K. Bond, Larry W. Hurtado: Eerdmans, 2015.

Leadbetter, Bill. 'Constantine and the Bishop: The Roman Church in the Early Fourth Century'. *Journal of Religious History* 26, no. 1 (2002): 1–14.

Lo, Wei, and Wei Luo. *Ezekiel in Revelation: Literary and Hermeneutic Aspects*. University of Edinburgh, 1999.

Marcus, Joel. 'Birkat Ha-Minim Revisited'. *New Testament Studies* 55, no. 4 (n.d.): 523–51.

Maurizio, L. 'Anthropology and Spirit Possession: A Reconsideration of the Pythia's Role at Delphi'. *The Journal of Hellenic Studies* 115 (1995): 69–86.

Merlini, Marco. 'The Pagan Artemis in the Virgin Mary Salutation at Great Lavra, Mount Athos'. *The Journal of Archaeomythology* 7 (2011): 106–80.

Morris, Benny. *The Thirty-Year Genocide: Turkey's Destruction of Its Christian Minorities, 1894–1924*. Illustrated edition. Cambridge, Massachusetts: Harvard University Press, 2019.

Parks, Tim. *Medici Money: Banking, Metaphysics and Art in Fifteenth-Century Florence*. Profile Books, 2013.

Parvis, Sara. 'Perpetua'. *The Expository Times* 120, no. 8 (1 May 2009): 365–72.

Ricoeur, Paul. *Time and Narrative*. Vol. 2. University of Chicago Press, 1990.

Shoemaker, Stephen. 'The Cult of the Virgin in the Fourth Century: A Fresh Look at Some Old and New Sources', 71-87. In *Origins of the Cult of the Virgin Mary*. Ed. By Maunder, Chris. Bloomsbury Academic, 2008.

Sobczak, Kamil. 'Transition from the Temple of Jupiter to the Great Mosque of Damascus in Architecture and Design'. *Studia Ceranea* 5 (2015).

Strelan, Rick. *Paul, Artemis, and the Jews in Ephesus*. Walter de Gruyter GmbH & Co KG, 2014.

Tataki, Argyro B. 'Nemesis, Nemeseis, and the Gladiatorial Games at Smyrna'. *Mnemosyne* 62, no. 4 (2009): 639–48.

Taylor, Deborah Furlan. 'The Monetary Crisis in Revelation 13:17

and the Provenance of the Book of Revelation'. *The Catholic Biblical Quarterly* 71, no. 3 (2009): 580–96.
Teitler, H. C. 'Ammianus, Libanius, Chrysostomus, and the Martyrs of Antioch'. *Vigiliae Christianae* 67, no. 3 (1 January 2013): 263–88.
Thompson, Leonard L. *The Book of Revelation: Apocalypse & Empire*. New edition. New York: Oxford University Press, 1997.
Thompson, Leonard L. 'The Martyrdom of Polycarp: Death in the Roman Games'. *The Journal of Religion* 82, no. 1 (1 January 2002): 27–52.
Trevett, Christine. 'Apocalypse, Ignatius, Montanism: Seeking the Seeds'. *Vigiliae Christianae* 43, no. 4 (1989): 313–38.
Wypustek, Andrzej. 'Magic, Montanism, Perpetua, and the Severan Persecution'. *Vigiliae Christianae* 51, no. 3 (1997): 276–97.
Yamauchi, Edwin M. *New Testament Cities in Western Asia Minor: Light from Archaeology on Cities of Paul and the Seven Churches of Revelation*. Wipf and Stock Publishers, 2003.

HISTORICAL SOURCES

Augustine of Hippo, *The City of God*
Eusebius, *The Church History*
Ignatius, *The Epistle to the Philadelphians*
Irenaus, *Against Heresies*
Marcellinus, *Res Gestae*
Protoevangelium of James
Sozomen, *Ecclesiastical History*
Suetonius, *The Lives of the Caesars*
Tacitus, *The Annals*
Tertullian, *Ad Martyras*
Tertullian, *Apologeticus*
The Martyrdom of Polycarp
The *Passion of Saint Perpetua, Saint Felicitas, and Their Companions*
Theodosian Code

OTHER BOOKS BY MARKO JOENSUU

Five Movements: Winning the Battle for Your Prophetic Gift
Supernatural Love: Releasing the Compassion of Jesus Through the Gifts of the Spirit
Cloud 913

With Rami Kivisalo
The Red Scorpion: A True Russian Mafia Story

www.ingramcontent.com/pod-product-compliance
Lightning Source LLC
Chambersburg PA
CBHW032223080426
42735CB00008B/692